Ita

www.pocketessentials.com

Italian Cinema
Arthouse to Exploitation

Barry Forshaw

www.pocketessentials.com

This edition published in 2006 by Pocket Essentials
P.O.Box 394, Harpenden, Herts, AL5 1XJ
www.pocketessentials.com

© Barry Forshaw 2006

The right of Barry Forshaw to be identified as author of this work has been asserted
in accordance with the Copyright, Designs and Patents Act 1988.

All rights reserved. No part of this book may be reproduced, stored
in or introduced into a retrieval system, or transmitted, in any form
or by any means (electronic, mechanical, photocopying, recording or
otherwise) without the written permission of the publishers.

Any person who does any unauthorised act in relation to this publication
may be liable to criminal prosecution and civil claims for damages.

A CIP catalogue record for this book is available from the British Library.

ISBN 1 904048 55 2
EAN 978 1 904048 55 8

2 4 6 8 10 9 7 5 3 1

Typeset by Avocet Typeset, Chilton, Aylesbury, Bucks
Printed and bound in Great Britain by Cox & Wyman, Reading

Acknowledgement

To Judith, without whom…

Contents

1. Introduction — 9
2. Neorealism – Key Directors — 16
3. Neorealism – Two Key Films — 30
4. Personal Cinema: Fellini, Antonioni and Others — 34
5. Personal Cinema – Key Films — 49
6. Gialli – Key Films — 73
7. The Italian Western: Sergio Leone and Sergio Corbucci — 88
8. Italian Cinema: The Films — 103
9. Key Film Stars — 137

Index — 155

Introduction

Is sexuality the key to Italian cinema? From the unbridled sensuality of the orgy scenes in silent Italian cinema, through a topless Sophia Loren in a 1950s historical epic, to the image of Silvana Mangano, her skirt provocatively tucked into her underwear in the neorealist classic *Riso Amaro* (*Bitter Rice*), up to the erotic obsessions of Fellini and the more cerebral but still passion-centred movies of Antonioni, eroticism is ever-present. And then there's the popular Italian cinema: the acres of tanned flesh (both male and female) on offer in the many sword and sandal epics of the peplum era, through to the inextricable mix of sexuality and violence in the *gialli* of such directors as Mario Bava and Dario Argento. The latter may be said to be the final exhausted sigh of Italian concupiscence: a full-on *liebestod* in which death and sex meet in a blood-drenched, orgasmic finale.

Of course, there's far more to the genius of Italian cinema than this one motivating factor and, while the industry may be in abeyance today, its history represents one of the most glorious and energetic celebrations of the medium of cinema that any nation has ever offered. For many years, this astonishing legacy was largely unseen, but the DVD revolution is making virtually everything available, from Steve Reeves' muscle epics to long-unseen Italian art house movies, the latter often known to cinephiles by name only. The element of social commitment, often a key theme in neorealism, gave way as the years progressed to delirious experiments with other genres (often with a strongly surrealistic overtone), but the one characteristic that most of the great (and not so great) Italian movies have in common is the sheer individualism of the directors. And this applies to the populist moviemakers, as much as to the giants of serious cinema. While Federico Fellini, Luchino Visconti and Michelangelo Antonioni have rightly assumed their places in the pantheon, such talented popular *auteurs* as Sergio Leone have acquired a copper-bottomed following over the years, after the almost derisory reaction that their otherwise highly successful movies initially received – mainly due to the fact that Leone and Co. were using a popular genre, the Western, and doing something with it that no American director would dare to do, so radical was the rethink.

With the astonishing contributions over the centuries to the world of the arts (notably painting) that Italy was responsible for, it was hardly surprising that early silent Italian films were shot through with the same visual richness as the great works of such painters as Veronese and Caravaggio. Italian silent cinema is, of course, best remembered as being a great flowering of the epic and historical costume drama, notably the swarming, extras-packed Roman epics. *La Presa di*

Roma (*The Taking of Rome*) in 1905 is often celebrated as the first important narrative movie, with its plot of the breaching of Porta Pia by Italian troops in the nineteenth century handled with great panache. A synthesis with the other arts was evident in the provision for music to accompany this film (this was, of course, the era of Respighi, whose highly coloured music is often disparagingly referred to as being like film music, as if that were the most deadly of criticisms).

Directors such as Giovanni Pastrone (born in 1883) showed an exuberant grasp of cinema in *La Caduta di Troia* (*The Fall of Troy*) in 1910, which demonstrated tremendous assurance in its use of massive crowds within equally massive sets. The same director's *Cabiria* (1914), possibly the best known of all Italian silent films, and Mario Caserini's *Gli Ultimi Giorni di Pompei* (*The Last Days of Pompeii*) in 1913, sounded a theme that was to reoccur in the grand days of the peplum epics. Few later versions of these epic themes had quite the panache of Pastrone's and Caserini's work. *Cabiria* was extensively hand-tinted (a technique utilised most notably in the US with Lon Chaney's *The Phantom of the Opera*), and the staging of such scenes as that in which the heroine Cabiria is to be sacrificed to Moloch, the Carthaginian god, transcends (even to this day) the limitations of the silent era, and is still awe-inspiring.

Other elements that were to feature throughout the history of Italian cinema are also handled with great assurance here: elaborate special effects and cinematic trickery that created an epic sense of scale from limited resources. Italian audiences of the day flocked to these immense epics, and it is a testament to their ambition that their characterisation is still more subtle than one would expect of the era (although it is necessary for the modern viewer to grit their teeth through some semaphore-style silent film acting).

The film also marked the appearance of an iconic figure who was to feature (along with his myriad progeny) in many muscleman films of the 1960s, the super-strong hero Maciste. In *Cabiria*, he was played by the non-actor Bartolomeo Pagano, a strapping Genoan dockworker who became a star after his appearance in the film. Maciste was a tremendous hit with audiences, and he later reappeared fighting insuperable odds in many Italian epics of the 1960s, although his films would be retitled in the US and Britain, as non-Italian audiences were not familiar with the character: Maciste often became Hercules or Goliath.

Rather like the British cinema, the Italian cinema enjoyed periods of success followed immediately by hardship and crisis. A particularly swingeing economic crisis decimated the industry after the First World War, despite the fact that Italian films had been selling successfully in the American market. The films, however, continued to be made for appreciative local audiences, often built around the burgeoning star system, carefully cultivated by the filmmakers of the day. And while these stars (such as the charismatic Lidia Borelli) are little known today, the acting style employed is often surprisingly low-key and modern, as witnessed by Borelli's seductive performance in Mario

Caserini's *Ma l'Amore Mio Non Muore* (*Love Everlasting*, 1913). The sexuality of the films of this era is often surprisingly up-front; *Il Serpente* (*The Serpent*, 1919) is Roberto Roberti's erotic epic, full of imagery that remains deeply sensuous even to this day. The silent era was dominated by celebrated actresses such as Maria Giacobini and Diana Karenne, with some equally charismatic male stars making an impression.

The other arts continued to influence the cinema, and often various movements attempted to utilise the medium for their own purposes, such as the Italian Futurists. After Marinetti's celebrated manifesto (which took the art world by storm when it appeared in *Le Figaro* in 1909), it was only natural that the Futurists would be fascinated by the apparatus of cinema, with their preoccupation with the interaction of movement, the human figure and machinery. The essay 'The Futurist Cinema' (September 1916) made a strong plea for the cinema to embrace its essentially visual nature and become both impressionistic and dynamic.

Certainly, the darkest days of the Italian nation were the fascist era, and if Italian cinema of the day simply provided no more than escapism, there were (inevitably) few chances for the directors to do much else. Various sloe-eyed Lolitas seduced their male co-stars, Maciste battled various nemeses (both natural and supernatural). The dark days began in earnest in 1934 with the appointment of Luigi Freddi as head of the Direzione Generale per la Cinematografia, which was as sympathetic to the fascist movement as Freddi himself. A fund for the creation of Italian films was created, and one of the key elements of Italian cinema also dated from this period: the now famous film complex Cinecittà, which no less a figure than Mussolini himself opened in April 1937. As Italy continued to be ruled by a fascist government (from the 1920s to the 1940s), Mario Camerini was a key figure in this period. His *Rotaie* (*Rails*, 1929) was a powerful study of love, which avoided dealing with the political realities of the day, as did Alessandro Blasetti with *Sole* (*Sun*, 1929), now a lost film. Blasetti made an important historical spectacle in *Palio* (1932), which dealt with the effects of Garibaldi's invasion of Sicily on ordinary individuals of the period.

Looked at today, refreshingly few of the films produced during the fascist period show the crushing political orthodoxy one might expect (far less so, for instance, than the endless paeans of praise to Stalin made under duress by Russian directors after the communist revolution). Such films as Augusto Gianina's *L'Assedio di Alcazar* (*The Siege of Alcazar*) described a fascist victory (Franco's forces fighting the far greater numbers of a republican army), and the award of a Mussolini prize at the Venice film festival in 1937, hardly covers the film with glory, looked at from the present era.

But on the horizon was Roberto Rossellini's *Roma, Città Aperta* (*Rome, Open City*, 1945) which added a new level of sophistication and ambition to the Italian cinema, and took it far beyond the kind of material produced by the journeymen directors of Mussolini's regime. After Il Duce's fall in 1943, Rossellini produced such films as *Un Pilota Ritorna* (*A Pilot Returns*, 1942) and while still recognisably a propaganda piece, the Rossellini of the future was clearly in evidence.

Similarly, the aristocratic Luchino Visconti had been given a book that greatly impressed him, a French translation of James M Cain's *The Postman Always Rings Twice*. From this he would make one of the great Italian films of sexuality and violence, *Ossessione* (*Obsession*, 1942), and the inglorious recent past of the Italian cinema quickly receded. An explosion of filmmaking was in the offing, with all genres up for grabs. But the overriding preoccupation for most directors of the period, whether they were from working or middle-class backgrounds (or from a more aristocratic upbringing, such as Visconti), was the life of the common man. And some of the greatest films produced in Italy would result from this preoccupation, before audiences and directors tired of realism and yearned for colour, spectacle and unbridled sexuality. And the industry was crammed with filmmakers perfectly prepared to give audiences just what they wanted – even if it upset the all-powerful Catholic Church.

Neorealism – Key Directors

Sexuality is certainly the wellspring of one of the key documents of Italian neorealism, Luchino Visconti's *Ossessione* (*Obsession*, 1942), a sultry, highly eroticised version of James M Cain's *The Postman Always Rings Twice* that made the Hollywood version with John Garfield and Lana Turner seem a very buttoned up affair indeed (it was to be many years before Jack Nicholson and Jessica Lange would put table-top intercourse back into the tale). Visconti's *Ossessione* (with Massimo Girotti and Clara Calamai) is a key film in the history of Italian cinema, as it functions on so many different levels. The director had been associated with the writers and filmmakers of the journal *Cinema* (which was in fact a project put together by Vittorio Mussolini, the dictator's son) and he had already set down a manifesto which included a swingeing attack on standard Italian cinema of the day (entitled 'Cadavers') and which also articulated his feelings that the everyday life of men and women should be encapsulated in cinema, with a keen and subtle response to the locales in which human dramas were placed. The Minister of Popular Culture, Alessandro Pavalini, had rejected a proposed film of a Verga short story,

Gramigna's Lover, as it did not conform to the rules of fascist cinema. As a replacement project, Visconti considered Melville's *Billy Budd*, later filmed by Peter Ustinov, but finally opted for a film based on a French translation he'd read of Cain's *Postman* with its betrayal, sexuality and resolutely blue-collar characters. With the assistance of such colleagues as Giuseppe de Santis (who would later become a director himself), Visconti relocated the book to a sultry Italy, and took its classic tale of a couple who murder the woman's husband for his money and then fall out in an orgy of what ultimately proves to be lethal squabbling, and made it quintessentially Italian. The characters of Frank, Cora and Nick become Gino, Giovanna and Bragana (the latter characterised as an admirer of Verdi – an element that would not have displeased the opera-loving Cain). But the principal change to the novel was the removal of focus on the District Attorney and Frank's lawyer. In their place, Visconti created the homosexual Lo Spagnolo (the Spaniard), an early example of the gay director's own interest in homosexuality. The first-person narrative of the novel was jettisoned for a cool and dispassionate camera style that brilliantly rendered the baked, arid landscapes with (for the time) striking novelty. All the elements were brought together in a synthesis which was quite unlike anything else that had previously been attempted in Italian cinema. There are details that are far more striking than anything to be found in the Tay Garnett US version of the story (such as Gino's shaving with a straight razor, while in the background Giovanna massages the overweight body of her husband – as a harbinger of a violent death that would ensue, this is a perfect visual metaphor). The film created something of a sensation, particularly among such critics as André Bassin, and it was clear that Visconti had elevated the squalid sex and violence of Cain's plot into something that was genuinely operatic yet never over the top.

Needless to say, the film created a scandal in the censorious atmosphere of Mussolini's Italy. Il Duce himself looked at the film, but did not halt its distribution. It was left to his son Vittorio, who famously denounced the film (after a public screening) with the words 'this is not Italy'. Perhaps it was not the Italy of the Fascists, but the humanity and power of the film survives after so many of the dull propaganda pieces of the day have fallen by the wayside.

There is much debate about what the term 'neorealism' in Italian cinema actually means, and probably the safest approach is to regard it as a portmanteau concept in which various elements were treated: a committed, generally left-wing approach to the problems of society; deliberately de-glamorised pictures of Italian life, in films that were often cast with non-actors (sometimes shored up with professionals such as Anna Magnani); and, in general, working class rather than middle class milieux and concerns. There is little question that the form grew up as a reaction to fascism, but its deliberately 'non-artificial' aspects are actually underpinned by a passionate approach to human problems that frequently reminds the viewer that Italy is the country of grand opera (in Italian opera, the *verismo* movement had produced operas with similar concerns, such as Mascagni's *Cavalleria Rusticana* and Leoncavallo's *I Pagliacci*). The key figures in the movement were Roberto Rossellini, Vittorio De Sica, the aforementioned Visconti and, although he is not strictly a neorealist director, the early films of Federico Fellini. All shared a passionate concern for conveying the realities of quotidian working class existence (remarkable in the case of Visconti, with his aristocratic background). Themes that concerned these directors included ones which were then topical: the effects of the war and the resistance activities of the partisans; the degrading of the workforce through unemployment; and the aspects of municipal corruption that destroyed the quality of life for so many Italian working men and women. Rossellini's *Roma, Città Aperta* (*Rome, Open City*, 1945) was a major box-office success and demonstrated that the movement could be popular as well as revolutionary. Similarly, the director's *Paisà* (1946) and De Sica's *Ladri di Biciclette* (*Bicycle Thieves*, 1948) enjoyed popular as well as critical acclaim, as did De Santis's *Riso Amaro* (*Bitter Rice*, 1949). But, generally speaking, the movement enjoyed more critical acclaim and mainstream Italian audiences still preferred escapism (either of the Hollywood variety or via their own home-grown imitations) to depictions of the lives that many of them were living.

But these films (and such classics as Rossellini's *Germania, Anno Zero* [*Germany, Year Zero*, 1947] and De Sica's *Sciuscia* [*Shoeshine*, 1946]) absolutely defined the movement and have proved timeless, still having a powerful impact today when the sociological concerns of the directors are now history. With *Roma, Città Aperta*, Rossellini threw down a gauntlet for the cinema of the day. In many ways it was a classic example of guerrilla filmmaking, with most of the shooting taking place on location, and even the film stock being obtained by clandestine means. Rossellini did not enjoy the luxury of access to daily rushes, and all the sound in the film is post-synched (as there was no budget for any live sound recording) – in this, however, the film fell in with a long-established Italian technique, where most dialogue is looped in the studio later. The film itself is a striking synthesis of radically different techniques: the documentary aspects of the film are set against operatically heightened emotions, and the partisan struggle against the German invaders is conveyed with both a dispassionate realism and an attention to violence and tension that makes most contemporary Hollywood (or British) efforts seem contrived indeed. The characters are a partisan priest, Don Pietro (Aldo Fabrizi), who fights alongside partisan leader Manfredi (Marcel Pagliero) against the Nazis. Manfredi, however, is doomed when his treacherous lover Marina (Maria Michi) betrays him to the Germans (in the person of the psychopathic Major Bergman). Apart from Fabrizi's astonishingly nuanced performance, however, the character most viewers remember is, of course, the working class Pina (played by the incandescent Anna Magnani) who is a friend of Manfredi. Her fate in the film at the hands of the Nazis, along with that of the brave priest, remains as powerful an image as ever when viewed in the twenty-first century, and if the Germans are allowed little nuance, this is part and parcel of Rossellini's attempt to deliver his message with maximum force. The fact that he makes the Nazi Bergman homosexual in a further effort to convey his perversion is not, in fact, an action that can be attributed only to straight directors; the gay Visconti similarly treated several of his homosexual characters in an unsympathetic fashion, and it can perhaps be read in the same fashion as the treatment by such directors as Hitchcock of his gay villains – a dramatic truism of the day that may not meet today's standards of political correctness but that functions as a metaphor for transgression. Similarly, Bergman's colleague Ingrid is a predatory lesbian who is responsible for Marina's traducing of Manfredi, with her seduction by drugs and baubles. The pending marriage of Pina and the typesetter Francesco is a central image, making the final tragic denouement all the more powerful. But despite the fates of its central characters, there is a humanistic embracing of a possible future lying beyond the grim present. What still strikes the modern viewer is the richly drawn documentary surface, in which the more conventional film star performance of Anna Magnani is perfectly integrated. The suspense sequences still pack a considerable punch, such as the moment when fascist soldiers ransack workers' apartments in the Via Casalini for hidden resistance fighters. It is, though, the death of the Magnani character (shot in the streets by Nazi soldiers) and the cruel torture of Manfredi by a drunken Nazi that stay in the memory, and Don

Pietro's execution remains one of the most harrowing scenes ever committed to celluloid.

With *Paisà*, Rossellini moved even more resolutely into documentary mode, with a disjunctive narrative dealing with the Allied invasion of Italy. A voice-over and images of the movement of troops stress the documentary aspects, as does actual documentary footage bookending each separate section of the film. The individual episodes within this structure function brilliantly, and the relationship between the Italians and the liberating American soldiers is encapsulated in the very title ('paisà' is a demotic term signifying countryman or friend, and was the standard form of address between the natives and the American GIs). The most memorable episode involves a black GI, with his fantasies of a return in triumph to the USA finally playing out into a tragic denouement, as he realises that his status as a black man in a racist America puts him in line with the disenfranchised Italians he finds himself among. The structure of the film, which details various events giving a patchwork picture of the Allied invasion, is powerfully convincing. Rossellini's son Romano had died in 1946, and the director's method of dealing with his grief was to shoot another film, *Germania, Anno Zero* (*Germany, Year Zero*), which was dedicated to his son, and foregrounds a youthful central character in the film. After a somewhat portentous opening title, we are shown the destruction brought in Germany after the war, while a narrator tells us we will be watching a truthful vision of this large city lying in ruins. The construction of the screenplay follows a more linear line than that of *Roma, Città Aperta* and concentrates on the young Edmund, whose life with his father and sister is lived in a desperate fashion. His father is ill, and his sister obtains money from Allied soldiers for sexual favours. Edmund's brother Karlheinz was formerly a Nazi soldier and is in hiding. We are told that Edmund had denounced his father when the latter tried to end his involvement in the Hitler youth. Another portrayal of a negative, corrupt homosexual figure is presented in the Nazi schoolteacher Herr Enning, who sells records of Hitler's speeches to the soldiers using Edmund as a go-between. At the same time, he lectures the young man on the Nazi philosophy that he still passionately holds, and, working on the principle that the strong should survive while the weak fall by the wayside (one of the many simplifications of Nietzschian theory that the Nazis were responsible for), Enning persuades Edmund that he should murder his sick father. The ending of *Germania, Anno Zero* is as bleak as one could imagine. The effect of the film is occasionally schizophrenic, in that the documentary verisimilitude is undercut by the almost operatic horrors of the human story. The picture we are shown of ruined German landscapes remains immensely impressive, and the portrayal of the youthful Edmund (a perfect encapsulation of Nazi youth) has a strange, dual effect on the viewer. Again, the concept of perverted ideology being married to sexual corruption is aired in the figure of Herr Enning, but the detail is often more sophisticated than this schematic set-up might suggest.

After Rosellini, the other patron saint of neorealism

is De Sica. Vittorio De Sica was, in many ways, a more conventional filmmaker than his peers, and his success as an actor (initially as a romantic lead, then as a much-in-demand character actor in Hollywood films) chimes in with his more conventional approach. His first films as a comic actor do not wear well today, and when he took up directing in the early 1940s his true artistic calling was within his grasp. Utilising the screenplays of Cesare Zavattini, he created a body of work that remains impressive today. *I Bambini Ci Guardano* (*The Children Are Watching Us*, 1942) has a more structured feel than the more improvisatory qualities that are now seen as the hallmark of neorealism. The plot involves a woman's infidelity, which results in the loss of her son's love and her husband's suicide, but the presentation (seen through the eyes of the child) was remarkably successful, even though De Sica utilised everyday cinematic tropes to emotionally involve the viewer with his characters. *Sciuscia* (*Shoeshine*, 1946), the first major De Sica film in the neorealist canon, and once again it deals with the theme of the destruction of youthful ideals in the face of a cynical and bitter adult universe. Pasquale and Giuseppe, two shoeshine boys, save up to buy a horse. Unfortunately, they find themselves involved in a black market scheme when Giuseppe's older brother is sent to an Italian borstal for juvenile criminals. Giuseppe escapes and meets an accidental death, which, however, is blamed on Pasquale.

The tragedy through which the boys' friendship is destroyed is handled with masterly assurance by De Sica, and the cinematic language employed is much more sophisticated than that utilised by most Italian neorealist directors (not that they did not know how to use cinematic technique in a sophisticated fashion; they chose not to). The performances of the boys (Rinaldo Smordoni as Giuseppe and Franco Interlenghi as Pasquale) are astonishing, and make most portrayals of childhood in the cinema (particularly the Hollywood variety) seem hollow indeed. The horse (which is the boys' emblem of freedom) is a complex visual symbol that both opens and closes the film: its escape in the last reel is a metaphor for what has been lost between the two boys. De Sica is unsentimental about the boys – when Giuseppe is betrayed by Pasquale in prison (which is brought about because Pasquale is deceived into believing that Giuseppe is being beaten) the revenge taken by Giuseppe has disastrous consequences for both boys.

One aspect of neorealist cinema that now appears to have variable results (although it was much lauded at the time) is the use, by directors such as De Sica, of non-professional actors. The two non-professional children in the film give what appear to be remarkable performances, such is the empathy with which De Sica directs them. De Sica's own skills as an actor made him hyper-conscious of the artificiality that a professional can slip into, but the great performances throughout the neorealist canon (such as those by Anna Magnani) often throw into perspective the limited range of the non-professional players. However, the triumph of the method is to be found in *Ladri di Biciclette* (*Bicycle Thieves*, 1948), which is both De Sica's masterpiece and one of the defining films of the neorealist movement. It is discussed in the next chapter.

After *Sciuscia* and *Ladri di Biciclette*, De Sica presented his other great neorealist testament in *Umberto D* (1952). This was the director's own favourite film, which he financed himself, and its box office failure was a tremendous disappointment to him. At the time, it was viewed as sentimental and a falling off from the ideals of neorealism. But its reputation has subsequently grown considerably, and it is now regarded as one of his great works.

Pensioner Umberto (Carlo Battisti) is living a quiet and uneventful life until the series of disastrous events that we are shown in the course of the film. In a remarkable performance, Battisti presents the old man's life in a series of well-observed tableaux with both his pet dog and a youthful maid who lives in the same apartment. Battisti was a Florentine who had been a university professor, but such is De Sica's direction of this non-professional that it is impossible to think of him as a non-actor. The theme of the film is the position of the old in modern society, and it remains as pertinent in the twenty-first century as when it was made – particularly as De Sica keeps in check the sentimentality that occasionally creeps into his films. This strategy is most marked in the presentation of Umberto D himself, who is often an unsympathetic and bad-tempered character.

While *Ladri di Biciclette* had revelled in its *non pareil* exterior photography, De Sica set himself the problems of filming indoors, but the Cinecittà interiors are brilliantly designed. This utilisation of studio resources never undercuts the neorealist agenda of the film, and the visual effects are extremely well handled. While *Ladri di Biciclette* will remain De Sica's signature work, it seems more and more likely that *Umberto D* will join it in the pantheon of neorealist masterpieces. Zavattini's writing, too, is perfectly in accord with the director's vision.

Despite Luchino Visconti's aristocratic background, he demonstrated by his actions his concern for all the inhabitants of his country when he took part in active resistance against the occupying Germans, by helping Allied prisoners and offering refuge to partisans on his own estate. His film *La Terra Trema* (*The Earth Trembles*, 1948) was another key work that reflected these earlier political concerns. Eschewing any studio facilities, the film was shot in the most naturalistic fashion, utilising the inhabitants of a peasant village and even making the film using the (often impenetrable) dialect of the villagers themselves. This in itself was something of a political act, as the use of this dialect marked the director out from the establishment view of what was acceptable in cinema. The director utilised Italian subtitles in his own country, as the Sicilian dialogue was difficult to understand for northern audiences. *La Terra Trema*, apart from its own considerable virtues, also marked a launching pad for two of Visconti's assistants, later to become major directors themselves: Franco Zeffirelli and Francesco Rosi.

The film's subject was the bleak and difficult lives of the peasants, with the conflicts in a fishing family as the fulcrum of the drama. The son of a family has turned against traditional aspects of his trade (much to the irritation of his father) and takes a stance against the crooked authorities who exploit the fishermen and pay them insufficient amounts for their catches. When Antonio Valastro persuades his family to mortgage their home in order to buy their own boat, they find themselves having to fish in terrible weather, and a violent storm wrecks their boat. In the end, the son has to go back to the corrupt fishing authorities, who forced him into this situation, cap in hand. Despite the bleakness of his scenario, Visconti's film is still a testament to the indomitability of the human spirit – although it has to be said that, viewed today, the film has lost some of its once formidable power, and undoubtedly has longeurs for the modern audience. Nevertheless, the depiction of the difficult lives of the fishermen is conveyed with great sensitivity and understanding. What makes the film such an achievement, of course, is Visconti's distance (as a nobleman) from the lives of his characters; a viewer unconscious of this social division would undoubtedly assume that the director was either a member of or closely associated with the class he depicts, such is his sympathy for the plight of his impoverished fishermen.

However, despite its rich harvest of important and socially committed films, the neorealist movement had a finite life. Like later trends in Italian cinema discussed later in this book, all the directors had produced their finest work, and had made all the important points that could be made within the constraints of the form.

ITALIAN CINEMA

Italian cinema was ripe for another movement, one that would build on the innovations of neorealism but introduce a very different (though equally personal) vision, as expressed by some of the greatest directors in the history of the cinema. But before moving on to these innovations, let's look at some of the key films of the neorealist movement.

Neorealism – Two Key Films

Ladri di Biciclette (*Bicycle Thieves*, 1948)

Possibly the best-loved of all Italian neorealist films is Vittorio De Sica's *Ladri di Biciclette*, with its *non pareil* use of non-actors in the central roles of a father and his son. In fact, the power of this deeply affecting film is often down to the astonishing verisimilitude produced by De Sica's non-professionals, and it is a testament to his skill that it is impossible to imagine accomplished film actors producing better performances. Ironically, the film at one point could have turned out to be a standard Hollywood product: no less than David O Selznick suggested that he would put up the money for the film if De Sica was prepared to use Cary Grant as the desperate father (the mind boggles at the possible result – marvellous as Grant is in the work he did for such directors as Hitchcock and Hawks, his casting in *Ladri di Biciclette* simply doesn't bear thinking about). De Sica built on the achievements of *Sciuscia*, with another plot built around an important social issue. Antonio Ricci has been out of a job for several years, and finally manages to find a position as a bill-poster. However, the job is dependent on him owning a bicycle. The theft of a bicycle for most people would be an inconvenience; for Ricci it is a catastrophe. The film is basically an odyssey, as Ricci and his son Bruno travel all over Rome in increasingly desperate attempts to find the stolen bicycle. Ironically, the thief is found shortly after the duo visit a fortune-teller.

All of this is handled with tremendous assurance by De Sica, and the life of the poor in Rome is conveyed with maximum realism. As Ricci is pushed ever closer to the end of his tether, the scene is set for one of the classic moments in cinema: in desperation, Ricci is forced to become that most despised of creatures himself – a bicycle thief. His theft of a bicycle and his almost immediate apprehension by a vengeful crowd is as powerful as anything in cinema, as is the successive scene involving Ricci's son. Despite the air of improvisation, De Sica's film is as carefully structured as any Hollywood product, and the organisation of the crowd scenes is astonishingly adroit. The scene in which Ricci's bicycle is stolen is handled with the panache one might expect in a more outwardly polished product, but this is the art that conceals art: De Sica's achievement is to render his technique invisible. Interestingly, De Sica points up the artificiality of the Hollywood product of the day by utilising a poster for a Rita Hayworth film during a crucial scene.

André Bazin was one of many critics who hailed the film as a masterpiece, and even claimed that De Sica used Communist ideology in the film; this isn't quite the case, but there is no doubting the concern for working people that is at the heart of the film.

However, De Sica has a very different attitude to his workers than that of a contemporary director of outwardly similar leanings such as Ken Loach. Invariably in Loach's films most working people are presented as noble, with the authorities invariably as corrupt or foolish. De Sica has no such schematic illusions, and there is little sympathy between the impoverished protagonists as they struggle to obtain the few available jobs. In fact, De Sica's film contains an implicit plea for a change in society's values which remains as potent as ever.

Riso Amaro (*Bitter Rice*, 1949)

Giuseppe De Santis was, like so many filmmakers, a writer on film and produced celebrated work in the magazine *Cinema*. His experience with Visconti on *Ossessione* inspired him to produce his own work, and his first film, *Caccia Tragica* (*Tragic Pursuit*, 1947) was a drama about Italian partisans. However, it was with *Bitter Rice* that De Santis really made his mark and produced one of the defining works of Italian neorealist cinema. Ironically, a great deal of the film's success was its erotic charge (another example of the sensuality often beneath the surface in Italian cinema); the image of the seductive Silvana Mangano, her skirt tucked into her knickers, became one of the most famous images in cinema, and suggested to audiences worldwide that a more realistic eroticism was to be found in foreign films than in the neutered post-Hays Code world of Hollywood.

Riso Amaro strip mines similar territory to that of

Ossessione: a James M Cain-style plot of erotic obsession and violence. The film involves four protagonists. Doris Dowling is Francesca and Vittorio Gassman is Walter, a couple who have committed a jewel theft and escape on a train taking women to work in the rice fields of the Po Valley. Although they escape justice, great problems await them there. Francesca meets the charismatic Marco, an Italian soldier played by Raf Vallone. At the same time, Walter takes up with a woman working in the rice fields, Silvana (played by the sensuous Silvana Mangano, who ironically would later become an image of buttoned-up rectitude for such directors as Visconti in *Death in Venice*). Walter persuades Silvana to help him rifle the rice harvest, but at the climax of the film, Silvana shoots Walter, after discovering that he has given her paste costume jewellery, and then takes her own life.

While the film ostensibly portrays the day-to-day existence of women rice workers, who perform back-breaking labour under terrible conditions for a rice allocation and a handful of lire, the elements of melodrama imported from the American hardboiled genre create a strange synthesis in which a variety of styles are evident. While this fusion may look less successful today than it did in the late 1940s, there is no denying the impact that the film had (not least because of Mangano's revealing outfits) and even though the sight of Mangano's breasts and exposed legs was probably responsible for more ticket sales than the social comment of the film, De Santis was still able to make more cogent points (possibly because of this tactic) than in many a more worthy effort.

Personal Cinema: Fellini, Antonioni and Others

As the socially committed modes of neorealism began to show signs of exhaustion, a new and very personal form of cinema began to emerge in the Italy of the late 1940s and early 1950s. The directors who characterised this new trend (notably Michelangelo Antonioni and Federico Fellini) shared an interest in an intellectualised form of eroticism, though Antonioni's more glacial concept of sexuality owed something to the reigned-in eroticism of Alfred Hitchcock. The iconic Monica Vitti, muse of so many of Antonioni's alienated heroes, owes more to the buttoned-up but sexually charged charms of Grace Kelly than to the opulent, heavy-breasted signoras who populated the universe of Federico Fellini.

Antonioni had written scripts for several neorealist directors, notably Giuseppe De Santis for *Caccia Tragica* (*Tragic Pursuit*, 1947) and Roberto Rossellini for *Un Pilota Ritorna* (*A Pilot Returns*, 1942). As with the young Turks of *Cahiers du Cinema* in France, later to become directors themselves, Antonioni had made his mark as a writer for the influential *Cinema* magazine, and an article for that journal was responsible for his first venture into filmmaking, a documentary called *La Gente del Po* (*The People of the Po*) in 1943. The film (which had suffered war-time damage) was released in an abbreviated form in 1947.

A series of documentaries followed, and the cool, dispassionate narrative voice that Antonioni chose marked him out as different from both his colleagues and his predecessors. Another innovation that was peculiar to Antonioni was music. The scores for the great neorealist films had actually been among their most conventional elements, utilising the nineteenth century symphony orchestra in the fashion of Hollywood films of the day (an example of this is De Sica's *Umberto D*, scored in the style of Max Steiner), but Antonioni used dissonant jazz-orientated scores by Giovanni Fusco (later to be a recurrent collaborator) and Johan Sebastian Bach, with very different aims from simply pointing up the drama of individual situations.

As the 1950s started, Antonioni began to achieve a method of making films that bore traces of the work of Rossellini, but inaugurated a new, cooler and more demanding modus operandi than had been seen in Italian cinema before. His most striking innovation was a desire to explode the conventional boundaries of narrative, and to create a form of *mise-en-scène* that worked directly on the unconsciousness of his audiences (he had attempted to this style in his documentary work).

His first feature film as a director was *Cronaca di un Amore* (*Story of a Love Affair*, 1950), in which the

Antonioni style (certain throwback elements notwithstanding) marked out his mature vision as fully formed even in this early work. As with Alain Resnais in *L'Année Dernière à Marienbad* (*Last Year at Marienbad*, 1961) and *Hiroshima Mon Amour* (1959), Antonioni showed a far greater reliance on the elegant use of tracking shots, a device few of his neorealist predecessors had been disposed towards.

Similarly, actors were encouraged to underplay their emotions and allow the audience to fill in the requisite gaps. Ironically, this cool approach created a seismic reaction in film scholarship: while audiences were slow to respond to the new, more demanding aesthetic that Antonioni created, critics immediately recognised a major new talent at work, with a very different agenda from his predecessors. *Cronaca di un Amore* draws on the same American pulp territory as Visconti's *Ossessione*: the destructive effects of erotic obsession. Ferdinando Sarmi plays Enrico, a well-heeled Milanese engineer who becomes obsessed with the life of his young wife Paola (Lucia Bosé) and hires a private detective to investigate her. The investigator uncovers some uncomfortable facts: a girlfriend of Paola's died after a fall down a lift shaft, and her fiancé Guido (Massimo Girotti), who also had a relationship with Paola, disappeared soon after. When Guido becomes aware that he is being investigated, he travels to Milan to track down Paola once again, and passion is reignited between the lovers. The final results are disastrous for Enrico, who had set the whole course of events in motion.

Despite the relative conventionality of the narrative

(which, as a subject, might well have been filmed by a director such as Anthony Mann as a 1940s film noir), it is Antonioni's refusal to judge his characters that marks the film out as something different from what had gone before: we are allowed to view the characters without any directorial nudging, and (as was the case with subsequent films directed by Otto Preminger) a certain intelligence is presupposed on the part of the viewer in being able to pick an emotional response from an available range.

This respecting of the viewer's intelligence was something new in cinema, and Antonioni was to take the concept to even more rarefied heights. Another key shift of emphasis in Antonioni's film from its neorealist predecessors is the shift of class in the protagonists. The luxurious atmosphere presented here is upper middle to upper class, and reflects (for one of the first occasions in Italian cinema) a director being prepared to tackle the class with which he is most familiar, Visconti, of course, being the *locus classicus* of directors treating classes other than his own – although the latter was subsequently to deal with the aristocracy in such films as *The Leopard* (1963). Another innovation was the astonishingly beautiful look of the film, with each frame given the kind of painterly attention that would have been considered self-conscious during the neorealist period. There were parallels between the earlier movies (such as the casting of Massimo Girotti in a key role; he had played the luckless hero of Visconti's *Ossessione*), but clearly a new voice was on the scene.

The director's next important film was *Il Grido* (*The

Cry, 1957), the first of the director's films to be seen widely in the UK and the US. The film is the first serious treatment of a recurring theme in Antonioni: an odyssey undertaken by the central character in which layers of emotional truth are stripped away during a precise geographical progression of the characters. The protagonist here is Aldo (played by the American actor Steve Cochran), who works at a sugar refinery. His relationship with Erma (Alida Valli) is in trouble, and his emotional problems are at the core of the film. Valli was an interesting choice.

Cochran had of course enjoyed success in American films, but Valli's career stretched from such important American roles as Hitchcock's *The Paradine Case* (an unsuccessful film which nevertheless boasted a charismatic performance by Valli) and, of course, Carol Reed's *The Third Man*. Valli also made important contributions to French art cinema (notably Franju's *Les Yeux Sans Visage* [*Eyes Without a Face*]) and was even used totemically by Dario Argento in *Suspiria* (to be considered later). Her performance in *Il Grido* is one of her most understated — whether that was Antonioni's influence (he repeatedly requested that actors avoid anything that smacked of conventional actorly techniques) or the actress's own impetus, the effect is powerful indeed.

Erma tells Aldo that she has found out that her husband has died, and he assumes that the long-delayed marriage between them may now take place. However, she reveals that she has fallen in love with someone else, and the distraught Aldo leaves his job and takes his daughter Rosina (Mirna Girardi) into an uncertain future. As Aldo travels, he meets an old amour Elvire (Betsy Blair, another American import), who is clearly still in love with him, and has a sensuous encounter with the seductive Virginia (Dorian Gray), who runs a gas station. But these encounters are sterile, as is a tryst with the prostitute Andreina (Lynn Shaw), and a tragic ending awaits the hapless Aldo.

Il Grido is the first example of Antonioni's totally stripped down technique, in which all emphasis is subtle and understated. As Aldo undergoes his journey, the director's stunning but simple imagery perfectly counterpoints the decaying emotional life of his character.

The work that established Antonioni's pre-eminence in Italian cinema really began with the trilogy of *L'Avventura* (1960), *La Notte* (*The Night*, 1961) and *L'Eclisse* (*The Eclipse*, 1962) and would be consolidated by his colour masterpiece *Il Deserto Rosso* (*Red Desert*, 1964). The international celebrity that began with the English-language films *Blow Up* (1966) and *Zabriskie Point* (1969) remains a controversial period (not least because of the little seen *The Passenger* [*Professione Reporter*, 1965] with Jack Nicholson). Antonioni's work in the English language was considerably less assured than his earlier masterpieces, although all of these later films have their splendours.

But the first truly great Antonioni masterpiece was *L'Avventura*. This, of course, is the film that utilises what initially appears to be a conventional 'search' narrative – a young girl goes missing on an island and is searched for by her wealthy friends. But the plot is never resolved, and we never learn what happened to Anna (Lea Massari). Antonioni is less interested in the mechanics of plotting than in what the search reveals about his characters, principally Claudia (Monica Vitti), Anna's well-placed friend, and Anna's lover Sandro (Gabriele Ferzetti), who begin a tentative and guilty relationship during the search for the missing girl.

The Mediterranean cruise that begins *L'Avventura* suggests the sybaritic and disengaged lifestyle of its moneyed protagonists, but the experiences through which the director puts them shows how their comfortable existence conceals an emotional desert. The mystery of what happened to Anna is, to this day, something of an annoyance for the viewer. Sometime after watching the film it will resonate in the viewer's mind, and although it is clear that Antonioni seeks no conventional resolution, he nevertheless means us to be irritated by this lack of resolution – and acknowledge that life invariably refuses to conform to neat and ordered patterns.

The director's next film, *La Notte* (considered separately) took the strategies of its predecessor even further forward in its examination of the unfulfilled lives of its protagonists. But a certain reaction began to set in with *L'Eclisse* (*The Eclipse*, 1962), in which the abstract techniques of the earlier works were taken to the limits of what might still be considered a structured narrative.

Myriad examples of Antonioni's artistry abound in *L'Eclisse*, along with some of the coolest and most uninflected acting in Italian cinema, with a cast that included Antonioni's muse Monica Vitti, Alain Delon (looped into Italian as he was to be in Visconti's *The Leopard*) and Francisco Rabal (the actor who had done such sterling work for Luis Buñuel). And, of all Antonioni's films, *L'Eclisse* demands total attention on the part of the viewer — anything less than a rigorous approach will make for something of a tedious experience, but those prepared to make the effort will find their patience amply rewarded. The characters are typical of Antonioni in that they are primarily concerned with their own sexual and monetary desires. Vittoria (Monica Vitti) is a restive, vacillating young woman who emerges from an uncomfortable sexual relationship with an intellectual into a cautious affair with a young stockbroker. Alain Delon's performance as the stockbroker is deliberately pitched at a more energetic level than anything else in the film, and, while his scenes bring a kinetic quality notably lacking elsewhere, there is a strange meshing of gears between the scenes involving him and those depicting Vittoria on her own. Vittoria has seen what the neurotic frenzy of the stock exchange can do to people (her own mother is a hopeless victim through her dilettante dabblings) and is consequently wary of a deep relationship with the ambitious young man.

The progress of their relationship is identified through various symbols (the most recurrent of which is a piece of wood drifting in a rain-filled oil drum), but the film suddenly terminates in the middle of Vittoria's liaison. We are never told whether she and her stockbroker lover meet again. In fact, the final section of the film radically depicts no human characters at all – a truly audacious move on the director's part. Monica Vitti, under Antonioni's influence, invests the part of Vittoria with a calculated balance of restrained passion and inertia, and the world of the stock exchange is certainly conveyed with panache. As a picture of the aridity of modern life, the film is nevertheless demanding, and would give today's attention-deficit cinema audiences no short cuts.

Vitti was again the star of *Il Deserto Rosso* (*The Red Desert*). Interestingly, this first colour film by the director appeared in 1965 in the UK, in the same week as the first colour film of another celebrated master of cinema, Ingmar Bergman, whose *Now About These Women* offered a considerable contrast to the cool drama of the Antonioni film (Bergman's film is a frenetic farce). Both utilised colour with a degree of invention and understatement that was simply not to be seen in Hollywood products, and each established its own colour key, making points through the use of colour. But *Il Deserto Rosso* was by far the more ambitious of the two films.

The visual opulence of the film is astonishing, although the actual landscape depicted is a million miles away from the sumptuous, aristocratic setting of Visconti's *The Leopard*. The film is set in Ravenna, but Antonioni (as ever) avoids the tourist view of the city. His subject is industrial Ravenna, with its mills and refineries, characterless streets and dismal quays. These aspects of a less attractive vision of modern society nevertheless have their own *jolie laide* beauty, and the images are often memorable: a newspaper falls from a window and is trodden into mud. Carlo Di Palma's Technicolor photography is exemplary.

Giuliana (Monica Vitti) is a neurotic and troubled young woman having difficulty adjusting to her life after a car accident. And Ravenna is clearly not the place to bring about a change for her. Corrado, a friend of her husband (Richard Harris dubbed into Italian), appears to offer something new, and a tentative affair begins, rather in the fashion of Vitti's not particularly passionate relationship with Alain Delon in *L'Eclisse*, but the relationship goes nowhere as the characters never really communicate. The theme of non-communication is crucial to the film and encapsulated in a scene in which Giuliana asks a sailor (who clearly has no idea what she is talking about) whether or not his ship will take passengers.

There are many strikingly unusual examples of editing technique in the film, in which time is elided, with the entire narrative moving forward with these jarring cuts. The effect of this is often disorientating, which, of course, is exactly what Antonioni wants. As comparatively little is revealed about the characters, we find ourselves looking ever deeper into their impenetrable world – the effect is frustrating but immensely stimulating.

In the twenty-first century, the reputation of directors, thought unassailable in the 1960s and later, has undergone something of a sea change. While Godard's early films are still highly thought of, his agitprop Maoist works have totally fallen from favour. Ingmar

Bergman, once considered the greatest director in the history of the cinema, underwent a period of neglect, but his later chamber films (such as *Persona*) are now enjoying a reappraisal and his position in world cinema is assured.

Similarly, Federico Fellini was once considered the most important of all Italian directors, and his groundbreaking middle period works (notably *La Dolce Vita* and *8½*) were essential viewing. But Fellini was an over-prolific filmmaker, and as his later films diluted the spark of genius evident in their predecessors, his work began to seem like a parody of itself, and even his earlier masterpieces began to be retrospectively reappraised in a negative light. But looked at today, his films of the 1960s remain some of the most ambitious and interesting work ever achieved in the cinema.

Fellini had enjoyed an association with neorealist directors, but he never himself made a film that fitted within that genre, despite working on the scripts of many key films of the period, such as Rossellini's *Roma, Città Aperta* and *Paisa,* and Pietro Germi's *In Nome della Legge* (*In the Name of the Law*). His own agenda was something quite different, and as different from neorealism as it was from the work of his colleagues, Antonioni and Visconti.

Lo Sceicco Bianco (*The White Sheik*, 1952) was the first of his early films to establish his highly individual vision of modern Italian society. The comic narrative depicted in the film is built on illusion, but the imagery could not be further from neorealism, with the deliberate examination of the characters' novelettish concerns.

I Vitelloni (1953) inaugurates the plotless narrative that was to become Fellini's speciality. Seen at the time as a devastating analysis of the emptiness of provincial existence, it now seems like an accomplished precursor of such ensemble pieces as *La Dolce Vita*. The film draws upon memories from the director's childhood, with the five directionless young men at the centre of his narrative being the *vitelloni* (or, derisorily, the calves, as they are known in Fellini's home town of Rimini). The one we see most is Fausto (Franco Fabrizi), who is described as the spiritual leader of the group, and his relationship with Sandra (Eleonora Ruffo), the sister of Moraldo (Franco Interlenghi), another of the *vitelloni*, is central to the narrative, as the shotgun marriage and its subsequent betrayals put a strain on the life of the young men.

The observation of character and instant is as stunning as anything in Fellini's later work, but his ambitions were circumscribed when seen in the context of the later masterpieces. Certainly, these young men aren't going anywhere, but we are drawn less into their fates than we are into those of the characters who are played by Marcello Mastroianni in the later films.

Like Antonioni's *Il Grido*, *La Strada* (*The Road*, 1954) used an American actor, Anthony Quinn, and the result was similarly successful, with the post-synching of the dialogue handled with total aplomb. The film was notable for its use of the director's wife, Giulietta Masina, as the pathetic companion of the graceless strongman Zampano (played by Quinn). The film also established the highly fruitful collaboration with the composer Nino Rota, who became as much the musical voice of Fellini as Bernard Herrmann was for Hitchcock, or subsequently John Williams has become for Steven Spielberg. The theatrical aspect of the film, with its circus people protagonists, mirrored the film's gradual rejection of neorealist values. These characters are writ larger than those seen in Italian cinema before.

But the film that established Fellini as a key voice in Italian cinema was *La Dolce Vita* (1959), followed by the autobiographical *8½* (1963) and *Giulietta degli Spiriti* (*Juliet of the Spirits*, 1965), which featured a sympathetic performance by Giulietta Masina. Later films, such as *Fellini Satyricon* (1969) and *Roma* (1971) were rich in the imagery that had become the director's trademark, but lacked the narrative focus that made the earlier films so impressive.

La Dolce Vita, in which the feckless journalist Marcello (brilliantly incarnated by Marcello Mastroianni) wanders through a surrealist vision of Rome, is as much a picture of modern Roman society and attitudes to sexuality (embodied in the visiting foreign actress, the voluptuous Anita [Anita Ekberg]) as it is an attack on both the spiritual aridity of the period and the meaninglessness of religion (the film's celebrated opening shot of the statue of Christ being hauled across the city by helicopter remains one of the iconic images of Italian cinema). And the ruthless dissection of pointless celebrity culture is as *à propos* as ever.

Sprawling across the Totalscope screen in all its episodic glory, Fellini's epic essay on Italian morality is a vast, uneven work, which created a seismic division in critical opinion that persists to this day, although the striking of a new print in 2004 resulted in a slew of unalloyedly enthusiastic reviews. Ironically, the blasphemous sections would not raise an eyebrow today, and the rather decorous orgies were hardly pornographic even in the 1960s. There were those who found the meandering plot and episodic structure irritating, but many saw this as an exhilarating rejection of the linear narrative that had maintained a stranglehold on film for so long. Marcello is an amoral, attractive young journalist with a bevy of seductive admirers. He is quietly satisfied with his status and surroundings ('I like Rome, it is a dark jungle where you can hide yourself'). His is a happy, pointless existence that begins to pall as a series of incidents attacks his equilibrium, culminating in a rather tepid orgy. Mastroianni's performance is beautifully underplayed and sets off the often bizarre imagery perfectly. As so often in Fellini's work, his male protagonist is surrounded by adoring or sexually available females, and the performances of Anouk Aimée and Yvonne Furneaux are as well judged as Ekberg's brief but iconic appearance, famously wading in the Trevi Fountain, cleavage resplendent. Fellini's scalpel-like dissection of Italian decadence cleverly moves between the cruel and the operatic, and his love for the things he criticises grants the film its schizophrenic fascination.

Fellini's next film was the highly influential *8½*, discussed separately. Fellini's career continued to produce more autumnal masterpieces such as the almost plotless *Roma* (1971) and the anarchic *Prova d'Orchestra* (*Orchestral Rehearsal*, 1978), but it is undoubtedly true that when any history of cinema is written, it is his 1960s movies that remain his greatest legacy.

Luchino Visconti, a key contributor to the neorealist movement, produced his greatest work of personal cinema in *The Leopard* (1963), a massive, elegiac masterpiece (much mutilated in its day by its distributors), which enshrined wonderful performances by Burt Lancaster (as De Lampedusa's doomed aristocrat), Alain Delon and Claudia Cardinale. The film, which is only now available in the form that the director intended, can be seen as one of his greatest works, perhaps over-leisurely but always impressive in its encyclopaedic picture of a key period in Italian society.

Personal Cinema – Key Films

8½ (1963)

The reception accorded to *8½* in 1963 was even more divided than that accorded to his earlier masterpiece. Undoubtedly, the seeds of Fellini's later indulgence are clearly in evidence in this thinly disguised autobiographical tale of a director (Mastroianni again) unable to come up with the concept of his next film, despite the endless probing of those around him. Seen today, the excesses seem perfectly apposite to the theme, with Guido Anselmi a somewhat idealised portrait of the director, but with a certain wry self-criticism evident (notably in the reaction to the erotic opportunities presented to him). While trying to finish a science fiction film, Guido is fighting the distractions of friends, mistresses, producers, wives and critics (who come in for some considerable attention in the film, unsurprisingly). The format of the film moves between reality and fantasy, and the structure of flashbacks shades into uncertainty: the viewer is constantly disoriented by this approach. Another subject of the film is psychoanalysis, as Guido attempts to examine why he behaves as he does to his wife Luisa (Anouk Aimée) and to his opulent mistress Carla (Sandra Milo in one of the several larger than life portrayals that Fellini coaxed from her).

Guido is visited while asleep by his mother who takes him to a ceremony where he guides his father into a grave. His relationship with his mother is clearly more than the standard one, and the imagery of this sequence permeates the rest of the film. The film's set pieces are many and splendid, such as the mud bath sequence and the famous harem scene, in which a farmhouse Guido knew as a child becomes a repository for all the women he has encountered during his life.

A recurrent theme of this era of personal Italian cinema is the irrelevance of religion in this most Catholic of societies. The figure of the cardinal here offers conventional platitudes, which can give Guido no guidance.

When reviewing the women in his imaginary harem, Guido does not encounter the character played by Claudia Cardinale, who plays various roles in the film. She is a representation of the ideal woman to which Guido aspires, and is the one figure in the film who appears not to want anything form Guido.

To the accompaniment of Nino Rota's distinctive and inimitable score, the film ends with a classically Fellini-esque circus (a motif that was to become overused in his work, but is fresh and pertinent here). While later films such as *Giulietta degli Spiriti* may have utilised colour in a more delirious sense, this remains Fellini's most phantasmagorical film.

Boccaccio 70 (1962)

Many were enticed by the publicity for *Boccaccio 70*, anticipating a generous helping of cleavage from Anita Ekberg, Sophia Loren and Romy Schneider, which they got, although the contributions of the distinguished directors were less obvious. The three sizable segments of this promising anthology were directed by Federico Fellini, Luchino Visconti and Vittorio De Sica. Fellini's episode, 'The Temptation of Dr Antonio', was unpretentious and agreeable enough, but the satirical squib seemed like a watered down version of *La Dolce Vita*'s derisive onslaughts. Visconti was his usually impressive visual self (and provided the most serious entry), but the sombre mood of his sketch struck the wrong note in what was essentially a film of satirical squibs. And, alas, De Sica seemed to have been drained of all that made his work impressive, and 'The Raffle', while being superficially absorbing, was somewhat arid. However, the final effect of the film was agreeable enough, and notably diverting in the Fellini episode.

After some strikingly designed credits, *Boccaccio 70* opens with Fellini's 'The Temptation of Dr Antonio', which features Ekberg in an unlikely tale which devolves on narrow-mindedness and puritanical bigotry. Antonio (amusingly portrayed by Peppino De Filippo) is a vehemently radical self-appointed censor who objects to anything that conveys the suggestion that sex can be an enjoyable experience. His protests are generally ineffectual but cause much chaos. Antonio's moral indignations are inflamed when a massive hording depicting Anita Ekberg is constructed outside his apartment. Ekberg is seductively encouraging the public to 'drink more milk' (the lactation joke is similar to the one made by Frank Tashlin with Jane Mansfield in *The Girl Can't Help It*) and the episode concludes with a 40-foot Ekberg stepping out of the poster and clutching the terrified Antonio to her breast, *Attack of the 50 Foot Woman*-style.

The second episode is set in surroundings of velvety opulence and elegantly suffocating décor. This is Visconti's episode, 'The Job', which tells of a pampered young countess who discovers that her husband is involved in a call-girl scandal. Visconti accentuates the heavy, oppressive beauty of the countess's cloistered existence. He shows how her every need is satisfied by hovering servants and how she has become incapable of any profession in the world but prostitution, which she despairingly takes to at the end of the episode. Visconti's characters are dwarfed by the lushness of their surroundings, forever drifting through doors that lead to yet more lavishly furnished rooms, and their suffocating comfortable cages are impregnable. Fine performances by Schneider and Tomas Milian fail to give the episode more significance.

De Sica's colourful sequence with Sophia Loren as a fairground girl who raffles her body to drooling admirers is rewarding, but is a long distance from *Ladri di Biciclette*. Parcelled together, the three episodes are a pleasant enough *divertimento*, with several incidental voyeuristic *frissons*. Ironically, the final effect of the film is less erotic than the more reigned-in sensuality of more serious movies, such as those of Antonioni.

Il Cristo Proibito (*The Forbidden Christ*, 1950)

Curzio Malaparte's powerful film has worn well and remains as effective in the twenty-first century as when it was made. A young Italian who has been a Russian captive is released after the war and learns that his Partisan brother had been denounced to the Nazis and brutally murdered. Burning with a desire for vengeance, the young man, Bruno (Raf Vallone), returns home to avenge his brother by killing the man who denounced him. Malaparte's stark, unsensational film, with its cogent anti-war message, is photographed almost entirely in leisurely zooms and slow, probing panning shots. While these tactics reduce the level of tension, the final effect is mesmerising, even if the director's use of technique is self-conscious.

Accatone (1961)

In any discussion of personal cinema, the name of Pier Paolo Pasolini must figure: the director's complex personality – fiercely intellectual, Marxist, homosexual – informed a vision of cinema quite unlike any of his contemporaries, with his later films treating extensively (some would say obsessively) questions of sexuality. One of his first films to make an impression was *Accatone*. The film had a rocky start in the United Kingdom, with some of the most maladroit subtitling ever seen (later corrected). But the film created a great impression of realism, with a truthfulness in the rough and idiomatic dialogue. (The problem with the early subtitles was the attempt to render this slang in a crass 'mockney'.)

The film itself was as striking and impressive as anything produced by Pasolini's contemporaries, with the careful avoidance of anything that might seem glossy or slick. Arresting jump-cuts are utilised throughout, as is an abrupt use of music (a characteristic Pasolini was to employ throughout his career). The film is in some ways a more serious version of Fellini's *I Vitelloni*; 'accatone' is slang for deadbeat or sponger. The central character, played by the then non-professional Franco Citti (who later enjoyed a highly successful career for Pasolini and other directors), is one of this disenfranchised group who is married but leaves his wife to make her own way in the world with their children, while he sponges on the earnings of the prostitute Maddalena. When Maddalena is arrested, this hardly puts a crimp on his style and he begins to feel a real affection for the next woman with whom he takes up. At this point Accatone decides to get a job, but a single day of hard manual labour exhausts him, and he is soon taking up theft. The final results are, needless to say, tragic.

Gialli and Horror: Bava, Argento and Co.

The Italian horror film was probably the finest flower of the country's popular cinema, along with the stylish murder thriller (or *gialli*). The finest exponents of these fields (apart from the groundbreaking Riccardo Freda) were Mario Bava, Dario Argento and the less-talented Lucio Fulci.

Mario Bava

The hypnotic black and white cult classic *Black Sunday* (*La Maschera del Demonio*, 1960) easily transcends its indifferent acting and wretched dubbing to come across, even today, as one of the most poetic and lyrical of vampire movies. The performance of Barbara Steele as the vengeful witch who possesses the body of the young daughter of a nineteenth century nobleman is a triumph of charisma and presence over really rather crude acting. (Her fainting spells are one of several elements in the film one has to bear with to appreciate the virtues abounding.) Bava's fluid camera and brilliant use of atmospheric sets creates a haunting sense of unease in the viewer, and his years of experience as a lighting cameraman result in what has justly been called the finest monochrome photography in the horror genre. Of course, Bava's film is equally famous for its censorship troubles – details such as the spiked demon mask driven into Steele's face resulted in an outright ban by the British censor which lasted seven years. The heavily cut version held sway for many years, until the film was made available in uncensored prints, allowing viewers to fully enjoy the rich visual sensations with which Bava crams his film. Certainly, the cuts reduced *Black Sunday's* visceral impact – already modified by what films have shown in the intervening years – to a level that would hardly disturb a *Friday the Thirteenth* enthusiast. But provided you can make the requisite mental adjustments (there are other things one has to take a deep breath about – such as the fist fight that slows down an otherwise invincible henchman of the witch). *Black Sunday* will prove its reputation is justified.

House of Exorcism (*La Casa dell'Esorcismo*, 1972/75) and *Baron Blood* (*Gli Orrori del Castello di Norimberga*, 1972), resurfacing simultaneously in the UK, forcibly remind one of two things: how Bava's surrealistic, garishly-lit and mist-shrouded visuals greatly influenced the younger Argento and Fulci, and how often Bava came desperately unstuck with an inept script and miscast performers. *House of Exorcism* is, quite frankly, a sorry mess – an incomprehensible conflation of *The Exorcist* and any *Psycho* rip-off you care to name; Britt Ekland's exorcism at the hands of an ageing Robert Alda (father of Alan) neither shocks nor disturbs, and the blatant borrowings from Friedkin (the priest's guilt over the death of a loved one, for instance) underline how much more effective Linda Blair's demon (and Dick Smith's make-up) were at totally unsettling an audience. The sequences with a lunatic butler (played, tongue firmly in cheek, by a lollipop-sucking Telly Savalas) are marginally more successful, with several effectively gruesome murders. Of course, *House of Exorcism* is a recut, re-shot travesty of Bava's *Lisa and the Devil*, and now that audiences have had the chance to see the much-lauded original, his initial vision may be better appreciated. However, Savalas' lollipop-sucking 'comedy' performance sinks the original quite as irrevocably as it does the later version. *Baron Blood* (which appears to have suffered some censorship excisions) has Ms Ekland being menaced again, this time by Joseph Cotton as a revived aristocratic corpse. The actor's appearance and performance can only be charitably described as appropriate to the part, and further charity must be extended to the director by reminding oneself that this was the man who directed *Black Sunday*.

Of much more interest to the Bava admirer is his final film, *Shock* (1977) in which the director's acute sense of space is much in evidence, even if his eye-jolting colour schemes are more subdued than usual. Grisly *frissons* abound in this tale of a young woman pushed over the brink of sanity by a traumatic reconstruction of her past; a giant glass hand, for instance, adds to the edginess of the décor – particularly when it moves with no human agency. Dubbing is as grim as the plot developments, of course – and it has to be observed that much of the film was directed by Bava's son, Lamberto.

Blood and Black Lace (*Sei Donne per l'Assassino*, 1964) was Bava's tale of a masked killer prowling a fashion house, and remains the most influential *giallo* ever made. In the UK, the film was sometimes hooted off the screen for the achingly crass dubbing. But new Italian language prints have made it possible for viewers to feast on the visual delights afforded by chiffon, marble, and the director's cat-like camera. The crippling censorship cuts that truncated every murder are restored and the elegantly rendered tension is now unspoilt.

Bava had a hand, too, in most of the best sword and sandal movies that immediately preceded the horror boom. The muscleman epics (or peplums) were a mixed bunch, but Bava's exotically lit contributions as second unit director to Pietro Francisci's *Hercules* (*Le Fatiche di Ercole*, 1958) and *Hercules Unchained* (*Ercole e la Regina di Lidia*, 1959) starring Steve Reeves, added a lustre to these energetic comic strips, and Bava's own *Hercules in the Haunted World* (*Ercole al Centro della Terra*, 1961), with a vampiric Christopher Lee as Lord of the Underworld, has all the delirious imagination of his horror films. The other notable peplum, of course, is Vittorio Cottafavi's *Hercules Conquers Atlantis* (*Ercole alla Conquista di Atlantide*, 1961), with Reg Park as a lazy Hercules, and some stunning mise-en-scène.

Lucio Fulci

No genre director divides opinions as much as the Italian shockmeister Lucio Fulci – but as one who can find much to admire in his films (with *very* heavy reservations!). It's probably a little unfair to start with *Manhattan Baby* (also known as *Possessed*, 1982), which is really Fulci at his worst. Admittedly, Fulci's filmic virtues are in evidence – skilfully judged cutting at close-ups, unsettling placing of characters in frame, Argento-like use of music as a very important element. But they are buried here beneath Fulci's ubiquitous faults – ludicrously jumbled plotting, paper-thin characters and wretched dialogue. *Manhattan Baby* (not to be confused with the Isabel Adjani *Possession*) is not really characteristic Fulci – no shuffling zombies, little graphic gore (there is, unfortunately, some evidence of censorship cuts), but rather a vaguely *Exorcist*-style plot of the possession of a young girl by an ancient Egyptian force of evil. Some novel ideas emerge – a character entering the doorway of a New York apartment instantly becomes a staring-eyed corpse on the sands of Egypt – but the hard-to-swallow plot, and a total indifference to the fate of the characters, quickly sinks any interest. And without the blood-boltered *grand guignol* of Fulci's other films (zapping blue rays from a sinister amulet being the main special effect), there's little to divert along the way. However, let's be positive and turn to the more rewarding Fulci fare...

A Lizard in a Woman's Skin (*Una Lucertola nella Pelle di una Donna*), while by no means a total success, is a fascinating pointer to later ideas in Fulci's more blood-splattered epics. Basically a Hitchcock-style crime thriller set in a jaded 'Swinging London' milieu, it has several virtuoso set-pieces, such as a brilliantly shot chase in a deserted church which is almost a text-book example of how to utilise location shooting (as well as demonstrating a lesson Fulci has now apparently forgotten – how *one* flesh-rending knife thrust can be infinitely more shocking than a full-scale evisceration – the heroine's one ghastly wound in this scene reminds one of the throat-catching jump of Donald Sutherland's death in *Don't Look Now*). Carol Rambaldi's pre-*ET* contribution consisted of disembowelled dogs (for which Rambaldi had to produce synthetic models to save Fulci from outraged legal proceedings), but this isn't a Fulci 'splatter' movie and the difference is less noticeable than between, say, the cut and uncut videos of *Zombie Flesh Eaters* (*Zombi 2*, 1979).

And, of course, most people will know Fulci best from the latter film, a grisly Romero-inspired corpse epic in which state-of-the-art special effects of dismemberment and carnage offer a challenge to all but the most stout-hearted. It's in this film that Fulci's flat, comic-strip narrative grip flourishes — the plot (Ian McCulloch and Tisa Farrow stumbling through implacable, worm-infested zombie hordes) offers nothing of Romero's claustrophobic image-making, but is powerful enough in its own way.

The Beyond (*L'Aldilà*, 1981) is a slightly different kettle of corpses; here's the increasingly popular 'doorway to hell' idea given the Fulci touch with standard shuffling zombies. The usual inept dubbing overlays a curiously unreal Louisiana setting, and censorship cuts have reduced the parade of horrors (although, surprisingly, the crucifixion of the hotel manager seems untouched). Still, several atmospheric sequences are enough to justify the attention of Lucio's admirers. Despite his statements that he wished to concentrate on generating suspense in *City of the Living Dead* (*Paura nella Città dei Morti Viventi*, 1980) while playing down the horror aspects, Fulci provides more than enough graphic gore in his follow-up to *Zombie Flesh Eaters*. Certainly there is considerably less full-scale mayhem as the revived dead of Dunwich stalk their hapless victims, but the famous sequence of a girl being 'willed' to evacuate her entire inner organs through her mouth scores high in what Stephen King describes as the 'gross-out factor', and the zombies' favourite method of dispatching the town's inhabitants – clutching a handful of hair, scalp and brains from the back of peoples' heads – was (surprisingly) left untouched by the British censor (while performing excisions elsewhere). There is an undoubted *grand guignol* energy tapped at times, with the usual satisfying atmospheric tracking shots down misty, threatening streets. But it's not Fulci at full throttle.

While the climactic sequence of *The House by the Cemetery* (*Quella Villa Accanto al Cimitero*, 1981) is brilliantly sustained, it was never certain that Fulci had any grasp of the importance of structure in genre films. Certainly he has few equals in delivering body-blows of untrammelled horror, and there's a place for that in an industry overcrowded with no-talent hacks. But it isn't enough to talk about pure, plotless film (as Fulci does) to excuse cipher-like characters and attenuated story-lines – and if he is going to shore up his film with quotes from Henry James, something more than just dripping entrails, ripped jugulars and decapitations will be needed to justify these aspirations.

Dario Argento

One of the greatest causes for celebration in the DVD revolution has been the appearance of all the major films of the brilliantly talented Dario Argento – the ultimate *giallo* craftsman. His astonishing visual and aural assaults on the sensibilities of the viewer put the emphasis on the total experience of film rather than intellectual appreciation of a well-written script (Argento's horror films are definitely not for those who demand carefully constructed, literate screenplays!).

Usually to the throbbing, high-decibel accompaniment of the music of Claudio Simonetti's Goblin (his long-time collaborator), the films of this energetic Italian are a breath-stopping rollercoaster ride of painterly visuals and graphic horror. Argento's feature film debut, the poetically titled *The Bird with the Crystal Plumage* (*L'Uccello dalle Piume di Cristallo*, 1970), augured well for his career – a commercial success in 1970, it looks a fascinating dry run for many ideas to be more fully developed in later films. Tony Musante plays an American writer in Italy who witnesses a murderous assault through glass (prefiguring David Hemmings in the later *Deep Red* [*Profondo Rosso*, 1976]; he is trapped between sliding glass doors while attempting to aid the bleeding victim (Eva Renzi) – and this sequence seems to be the one people remember over the years – probably because Musante's subsequent tracking down of the black leather-clad murderer is handled with rather less panache than Argento was to develop in subsequent films. There are of course visual delights galore – a marvellously Hitchcockian chase of a yellow-jacketed hired killer (one of several loose ends not really tied up) that ends with a joke worthy of *North by Northwest*: a murder by razor that utilises sound as chillingly as Polanski did in *Repulsion* (a word would be in order here about Ennio Morricone's mesmeric score, cleverly used throughout) and the suspenseful siege of Musante's girlfriend (Suzy Kendall) in her flat – the murderer's knife cutting through the door invites another comparison: the demolition job done on a similar door in Hitchcock's *The Birds* – but this doesn't prevent the sequence from being claustrophobically pulse-racing. Quibbles apart, the film is essential viewing for admirers of the director – but I would suggest only after seeing his later, more assured features. *Deep Red* is stunning evidence that Dario Argento's delirious visual talents have been consistently in evidence, from his earliest films to *Inferno* (1980). A tortuous Hitchcockian thriller (with a relatively unguessable denouement), it is better constructed than *Suspiria* (1977) – the film it has most in common with – and the plot-spinning between the big, operatic set-pieces is better throughout. However, it is obvious that the director's real interests lie in the heady exploration of baroque architecture, in front of which his characters are gorily dispatched. David Hemmings, in a nod to his *Blow Up* persona, is almost witness to a murder, and, with the ambiguous aid of a young newswoman, threads his way through several menacing expressionist settings before, inevitably, confronting the deranged killer. The murders along the way are highly imaginatively staged – the death-by-boiling-water makes the similar sequence in *Halloween II* look thin stuff indeed. Several frissons are provided by Carlo Rambaldi's effects – the most shocking being decapitation by necklace and lift (not exactly a hackneyed demise – yet!).

The director's finest remains *Suspiria* (1977), the film that made Argento's name in this country. Two factors contributed to this: unlike his earlier films (and *Suspiria*'s successor, *Inferno* [1980]), the film received good West End exposure; and secondly, it justified the trumpeting. This was because *Suspiria* was unlike anything audiences had seen before – a visually phantasmagoric *tour de force* scored with a thumping wall-to-wall score by Goblin (which combined the sustained menace of more conventional symphonic scoring with atmospheric rock rhythms). The plot (minimal, to say the least) has Jessica Harper (of *Phantom of the Paradise*) as a new student in the sinister Friberg Academy in Germany; students and staff are decimated in spectacular fashion (the opening sequence in which Argento makes the heroine's arrival look like a magical passage into some Dante-esque nether world is followed by the most stunning double murder ever filmed, climaxing in a blood-spattered corpse crashing through a coloured-glass roof); finally, Harper's confrontation with the hideous, ancient witch Elena Markos – the diabolic force behind the academy – satisfyingly rounds off a film rich with splendid technical effects. *Suspiria* was described as the first part in a projected trilogy, of which only the second, *Inferno*, has yet appeared. *Inferno*, which had a limited release in 1980 (virtually buried by the distributor – their lack of faith being very short-sighted in the light of *Suspiria*'s financial success) is certainly a falling off from its predecessor, despite the film's virtues.

One of *Inferno*'s failings is its over-long running time

of 107 minutes, with a typically slim story unfolding in a rather leisurely way. The plot involves Irene Miracle as a young woman who discovers, via an occult book (shades of *Rosemary's Baby*), that the New York apartment house into which she has moved is one of three designed by an architect named Varelli for the sinister 'Three Mothers' of Whispers, Tears and Darkness (here we have the tie-in with *Suspiria*); the breathtaking sequence in a water-submerged room near the beginning, in which Mario Bava was involved, is unquestionably the best thing in the film – dream-like horror has never been captured so brilliantly on celluloid. Her subsequent death (savagely butchered along with a friend, Carlo) and its investigation by her brother Mark (Leigh McCloskey) comes across as a less tense reworking of *Suspiria*; nevertheless, as with any Argento film, some very satisfying felicities catch the eye – the bravura use of massive close-ups of locks as a character is menacingly pursued, and a grisly attack by rats in a park which has a marvellous twist at the end of the sequence. The score by Keith Emerson (instead of Goblin) is very effectively used – like Hitchcock with the inestimable Bernard Herrmann, Argento knows the immense value of music in suspense situations – even the chorus from Verdi's *Nabucco* is employed with great effect in the film. Certainly, the already converted will find much to enjoy in the film, and a less-than-perfect Argento is still streets ahead of a great deal of the so-called horror titles available on video. But perhaps the film seems more disappointing because of our high expectations, although the last reel of the film unquestionably *is* a disappointment – an unsatisfactory, slightly risible death of one major villain, and a very conventional conflagration to round things off. Notwithstanding these qualifications, *Inferno* is still a real achievement.

With *Tenebrae* (1982), Argento enthusiasts could savour, at their leisure, all the brilliant visual imagination of this Italian master of the horror film – nobody else in the field (not even Brian De Palma at his best) can wield a camera with such grace and applied power. Here, a contrived plot and perfunctory characters are effortlessly transcended by sequences such as the astonishing camera 'prowl' around the house of two murder victims. To the accompaniment of a pounding score by members of Argento's usual collaborator, Goblin, the director forsakes the supernaturalism of *Suspiria* and *Inferno* for a Hitchcockian plot involving a writer (Anthony Franciosa) plagued by a black-gloved murderer. Mention of Hitchcock is very relevant, as his ghost broods over the film (look at the sequence where Franciosa's agent John Saxon waits in a shopping precinct before a murderous knife assault: the steady accumulation of menace through innocuous sights and sounds – shoppers, children – is as brilliantly handled as Tippi Hedren's wait by the school-house in *The Birds*). The usual snooty critical disdain for Argento in the establishment press is to be confidently ignored by *Starburst* readers – just plug in your hi-fi, turn up the volume, dim the lights, and enter the terrifying Argento universe!

Luigi Cozzi

Once a despised genre (principally because of the crass dubbing they were invariably subjected to), Italian crime thrillers (or *gialli*) have undergone a major critical re-assessment, with their visual stylishness and imaginative plotting now celebrated. This is partly due to the availability of prints in the original Italian, and the effect is immeasurably more interesting – as *The Killer Must Kill Again* comprehensively proves. Cozzi's inventive *giallo* may lack the final ounce of plotting logic, but its dreamlike atmosphere exerts a considerable grip. The contribution of Michel Antoine's chiselled cheekbones (as the mysterious, unmotivated psychopathic killer) shouldn't be underestimated, as his physical appearance is as unsettling as anything Cozzi contributes in terms of direction. Unlike many a film in this blood-boltered genre, the more sanguinary moments are fewer (throttling is the killer's main modus operandi), but tension is screwed as tightly as one could wish – in fact, Cozzi's subsequently chequered career as a director is disappointing after the promise shown here.

Sergio Martino

When non-Italian audiences first saw his films, they thought they were watching films by Julian Barry or Christian Plummer, or even Martin Dolman. In fact, the Italian filmmaker Sergio Martino was (like so many of his comrades in the genre) obliged to work under a variety of pseudonyms. He would probably have preferred that some of his films languished under these pseudonyms, but Martino was one of the most energetic and vital of Italian genre directors. Born in Rome in 1938, Martino's varied film experience finally led him to his first job as a director, *Mille Peccati... Nessuna Virtù* (*A Thousand Sins and No Virtue*). Right at the start, this established him as a director of imagination, one prepared to take on the challenges of genre filmmaking and deliver something fresh and personal.

Martino is best known as a director of grisly *gialli*, but there are no genres that hold terrors for him, with westerns, tough thrillers and even ribald comedies on his curriculum vitae. In one area Martino is very much like his compatriots Mario Bava and Dario Argento: while never being as consistently inspired in his work as them, he is capable of truly vivid and engaged filmmaking, alongside some almost unwatchable, by-the-numbers work.

Martino came from a banking family, and became interested in films via his grandfather, Gennaro Grighelli, who directed early Italian sound movies. Martino's first move into the cinema, in *I Ragazzi dei Parioli*, called upon his acting skills rather than any directing talents, but he was also beginning work as a first assistant director. Martino's real break as a director came in the wave of *Mondo Cane*-style documentaries, with their crowd-pleasing mix of authentic grisly footage and reconstructions of the same. He then took the route that had tempted so many Italian directors: anodyne comedies (often with soft-core sexual situations). The director's brother Luciano produced several of these films, some of them starring Edwige Fenech (who was also his wife). She appeared in the 1976 film *Sesso con un Sorriso* (*Sex with a Smile*), which also featured Tomas Milian and wall-eyed English comedian Marty Feldman. But the director's true talent was to appear only when he moved into the genre that became his metier: the *giallo*.

Gialli are, of course, as famous for their unwieldy, slightly ungrammatical titles (both in Italian and when translated into English), and Martino came up with one of the most memorable in *Torso (I Corpi Presentano Tracce di Violenza Carnale* or *The Bodies Present Traces of Carnal Violence*, 1974). This, however, was shortened to *Torso* and is his best known film in this field and certainly one of the most assured and atmospheric entries in the genre (and, in fact, less graphic than its title might suggest, although recently more complete prints have become available). Using English actors such as John Richardson, Martino creates here an admirably disturbing piece, even if the identity of the killer is not that difficult to discern. The casting of Suzy Kendall as the menaced victim in this film – a function she also performed for Argento – is another reason for the film's success. Martino is also noted for *All the Colours of Darkness* (*Tutti I Colori del Buio*) in which he utilises his female muse Edwige Fenech as a woman under threat from a murderous cult. The strange, almost surrealistic narrative here is particularly memorable, and the film is a good example of Martino's intelligent use of both camera and *mise-en-scène*. Of course, along with his better films, there are also such duds as *Island of the Fish Men*, an item over which it is best to draw a veil. Similarly, his entry in the western stakes, *Arizona Si Scattenò... e Li Fece Fuori Tutti* was not particularly distinguished, coming as it did at the fag end of the genre's popularity. One of the director's more memorable westerns was *A Man Called Blade* (*Mannaha*, 1977), which was highly mannered (a western that looked as if it might have been written by Edgar Allan Poe).

Martino's skills had been honed observing the older maestro Mario Bava working on such films as *The Whip and the Body* (*La Frusta e il Corpo*), which was produced by Martino's brother, although his use of colour is notably less operatic than that of Bava. Probably the main influence on Martino was his contemporary Dario Argento, and *The Case of the Scorpion's Tail* (*La Coda dello Scorpione*, 1977) was clearly influenced by the great international success of Argento's *The Bird with the Crystal Plumage* (*L'Uccello dalle Piume di Cristallo*, 1969) and mimicked that film's tortuous (and slightly improbable) plot. Another less impressive entry in the genre by Martino was *The Strange Vice of Mrs Wardh* (*Lo Strano Vizio della Signora Wardh*, 1970 – yes, that's how it's spelt – also know as *Blade of the Ripper*). Although this builds a fair measure of tension, it remains no more than a merely craftsmanlike piece. The other main influence on Martino (apart from Bava's and Argento's *gialli*) was, of course, the subgenre of thriller that basically patented itself after Boilleau and Narcejac's *Diabolique*, with elaborate double-crosses and plots behind otherwise inexplicable actions. In between his cinema assignments, Martino worked for Italian television on such films as *The Scorpion with Two Tails* (*Assassinio all'Cimitero Etrusco* or *Murder in the Etruscan Cemetery*, 1982), although he was unable to place any kind of personal stamp on this work.

If, in retrospect, Martino's career is notable for more duds than successes, those successes show that, while as a director he was not in the same league as Argento and Bava, Martino was in fact one of the most interesting and imaginative makers of Italian popular cinema.

Umberto Lenzi

While the names of directors such as Bava, Argento and Martino have acquired the patina of a certain respectability, Umberto Lenzi has more notoriety attached to his name, notably for such films as *Eaten Alive* and *Cannibal Ferox*, grisly entries in the cannibal stakes that so upset the new censors back in the 1980s. But while Lenzi's career remains very hit and miss, there are things to be said for his work, and the recent re-emergence of such films as *The Killer Must Kill Again*, a tortuous *giallo* played out with real gusto, has reawakened interest in his immensely prolific career.

Lenzi began directing in 1961, and his CV now totals over 60 films. These range from adventures of the Batman-like super-criminal *Kriminal* in the late 1960s, a selection of punchy Italian westerns, and such *gialli* as *So Sweet... So Perverse* (*Cosi Dolce... Cosi Perversa*, 1969), and the deliriously named *Seven Bloodstained*

Orchids (*Sette Orchidee Macchiate Rosso*, 1972). And while violent action films such as *Free Hand for a Tough Cop* (*Il Trucido e lo Spirro*, 1976) and the gloriously sardonic *The Cynic, the Rat and the Fist* (*Il Cinico, l'Infame e il Violento*, 1977) were made with a craftsmanlike skill, they rarely exhibited the delirious, imaginative filigrees of Argento and Co. (although *Spasmo* (1974) and *Gatti Rossi in un Eyeball* (*Labirinto di Vetro*, also 1974) at times approached the achievement of the uncrowned king of the *giallo*, Argento.

Certainly, Lenzi is best known for his extremely grisly cannibal and zombie films, notably *Eaten Alive* (*Mangiati Vivi dai Cannibali*, 1980), *Cannibal Ferox* (1981 – also known by the title *Make Them Die Slowly*) and such zombie epics as *Nightmare City* (*Incubo sulla Città Contaminata*, 1980). These films all display the kind of uninhibited revelling in bloodshed that essentially brought about the Video Recordings Bill in this country. Looked at today, of course, their colourful special effects are far less convincing when seen in the crystal clear realisation afforded by DVD than they were in the grainy, panned and scanned video prints with which the films first became known. Lenzi attacked all of these various genres with great enthusiasm, and his success as one of Italy's hardest working exploitation directors cannot be gainsaid.

Gialli – Key Films

The Horrible Secret of Dr Hichcock (*L'Orribile Segreto di Dr Hichcock*), directed by Riccardo Freda

While the reputation of Freda's remarkable film is high indeed outside his native Italy, few people have seen the version that the director intended, owing to some mealy-mouthed censorship that removed a crucial element in the narrative. Rather in the manner of the American dubbing of Mario Bava's *Black Sabbath* – a sexual subplot was completely removed at the dubbing stage – the same sanitising process had already happened to Freda's movie. Bava was something of a Freda protégé, as the latter gave him his first chances to direct, and both men suffered this crippling form of censorship. So what is the completely unacceptable element in the original that caused so much concern? Necrophilia, no less. In 1962, such a subject was simply not acceptable in American and British cinemas. Freda's film begins with a man engaged in murky business over an open grave. Suddenly, a shadowy figure in a top hat appears and knocks the gravedigger unconscious. He opens the grave and the audience is shown the cold face of a female corpse. The intruder gently touches the face of the dead woman and then begins to run his fingers across her body. We are shown no more. The reputation of the film is probably due as much to what people know of its unorthodox central theme as to the stylishness of Freda's direction (although that is considerable in itself). There are also the performances, notably the English actor Robert Flemyng, who conveys the dark obsession of the driven Hichcock with cold skill (English audiences are always given pause by the apparent misspelling of Hichcock, knowing that the best known possessor of that name spelled it with a 't'). Bernard Hichcock is a doctor in nineteenth century London running a successful clinic with advances in anaesthesia ensuring fame and success. But he has a secret life, involving strange erotic scenarios with his wife Margaretha. In a darkened room, the doctor utilises his anaesthesia to create a necrotic state in her, which facilitates his sexual satisfaction. But things go wrong when he administers a lethal dose, and watches in horror as she dies painfully. Time passes, and Hichcock returns from a trip to Italy with a new wife. The house is soon prey to night-time visitations, apparently by a dead woman. Yes, to some degree we are in Laura/Rebecca territory, but the situation here is far stranger in terms of psychopathology. The trump card of Riccardo Freda's film is, of course, the casting of Hichcock's new wife Cynthia. She is played by the undisputed queen of the Italian horror film, the English actress Barbara Steele, who began her life as a Rank starlet. Along with Freda's delirious visuals, she perfectly encapsulates the gothic strain that is the director's speciality. As his roving camera prowls the house and strange things happen, the audience itself is lured into a kind of narcoleptic dream state, quite as hypnotic as that engendered in Hichcock's macabre love life.

Ironically, the more explicit bloodletting (and even nudity) of the Italian horror film in the 1960s had caused swingeing censorship cuts in films such as Bava's *Blood and Black Lace*, but the more subtle elements of Freda's work meant that the censorship practised on him related to what the characters discussed. While great Italian movies such as *La Dolce Vita* have been reissued in sparkling new prints, and various DVD companies have finally done justice to some of the remarkable horror films of Mario Bava, Freda's film, at the time of writing, remains unseeable, and enthusiasts of the director's work can only hope that it will finally be made available again in a form that expresses Riccardo Freda's vision.

Ecology of a Crime/A Bay of Blood/Bloodbath/Twitch of the Death Nerve (*Ecologia del Delitto*, 1971), directed by Mario Bava

Along with *Blood and Black Lace* (*Sei Donne per l'Assassino*), this is by far Mario Bava's most influential film on the cinema of other countries. Essentially an Agatha Christie-style murder mystery dressed up in the most graphic of killings, the film was virtually a blueprint for Sean Cunningham's *Friday the Thirteenth* series, with several of the imaginatively grotesque slayings lifted wholesale from Bava's film. Needless to say, the flat, unatmospheric milieu of the Cunnigham films is something that's very much that producer's own input, as Bava creates a typically delirious dreamlike state in his narrative even though *Ecology of a Crime* is hardly one of his finest efforts. The film begins with a particularly striking killing in which an elderly woman in a wheelchair is gruesomely hanged by a shadowy figure. Shortly after that, the killer himself is bloodily stabbed, but, as his body vanishes, the police are led to believe that the woman, a Countess Donati, committed suicide. A variety of people now descend on the bay where the murder took place, and lakeside sexual activities are soon the order of the day. But shortly afterwards, a strikingly grisly series of murders occur, and here Bava upped the ante in terms of graphic bloodshed, even compared with his own groundbreaking *Blood and Black Lace* (which underwent heavy censorship in this country). As various garden implements, etc, are used to cleave skulls and otherwise rend flesh, the motivation of the murderer would appear to be merely sadistic. But wait! This is an Italian horror film, and despite the frequent appearance of the supernatural, the most common motive for an orgy of bloodletting is invariably pecuniary – as is the case here. There are those who have read the film as a comment on human acquisitiveness, but Bava, tongue in cheek, is really enjoying doing what he does best – using the medium of cinema (after the fashion of Hitchcock) as a way of manipulating his audience.

The Black Belly of the Tarantula (*La Tarantola dal Ventre Nero*, 1971), directed by Paolo Cavara

The reputation of this film is fairly high, but that may be due to the fact that it was unseeable for several years. Regrettably, however, while flashes of inspiration are to be found, it is a fairly journeyman effort, with occasional moments of imagination illuminating the grim proceedings. The protagonist becomes aware that his seductive wife is being blackmailed over a pornographic photograph showing some adulterous dalliances. At the same time, a woman in an upscale health farm in Rome is brutally murdered, with another client of the salon being similarly despatched shortly afterwards. The method of the killings is notable: in the same fashion as certain wasps paralyse tarantulas before eviscerating them, a similar technique is being used here. Erotic elements are foregrounded here quite as much as any violence, with a nude Barbara Bouchet undergoing a sensuous massage before she is bloodily slaughtered. There are touches of Bava and Argento here, although the shiny black gloves of those directors are replaced by standard surgical ones. There is a particularly toothsome female cast, and Cavara orchestrates his suspense scenes with some skill. Finally, though, the effect of the piece is superficial.

The House with the Laughing Windows (*La Casa dalle Finestre che Ridono*, 1976), directed by Pupi Avanti

Another outlandish title, and in this case a suitably outlandish film to match it. Avanti has all the requisite visual skills for the *giallo* genre, and matches them with an ingenious (if absurd) narrative that functions intriguingly in its own right, rather than being a way of stitching together a variety of bloody set pieces. In 1950s Italy, a painter accepts an invitation to repair a fresco in a local church. The artist originally responsible for the piece enjoys a poor opinion in the town, and his fresco shows Saint Sebastian undergoing torture. Regrettably, as so often with representations of works of art in films, the piece depicted here simply isn't good enough to carry the weight that is assigned to it. The theory in the town is that the painter was showing the genuine agony of the male models he utilised as they were tortured by his psychotic sisters. The hero, Stefano, learns from his friend Antonio (who is subsequently murdered) about the fresco and about a house with windows that laugh. And as Stefano gets closer to the mystery behind the fresco, more bloodshed is the order of the day. Right from its opening sequence (in which a bloody stabbing is repeated seemingly *ad infinitum*), this is another piece firmly aimed at the exploitation market. But that's not to say that Avanti is not capable of a visual invention and thematic richness belonging to more ambitious films.

The Cold Eyes of Fear (*Gli Occhi Freddi della Paura*, 1971), directed by Enzo G Castellari

When *gialli* choose London as their setting, the results are often very odd indeed. But, as with Fulci, the results in *The Cold Eyes of Fear* add another stratum of delirium to the generally odd proceedings. The decadent Peter meets Anna, an Italian prostitute, in a Soho bar. When he takes her home, they find themselves at the mercy of a brutal young thug (with a particularly curious cockney accent) who takes them hostage. At the same time, Peter's father, an upright judge, despatches a policeman to the house with a note for his son. Surprising revelations follow. The policeman is not what he seems to be, and he has a relationship with the thuggish intruder. It soon transpires that the policeman is an even more terrifying figure than his brutal accomplice, a convicted criminal whose agenda is bloody revenge on Peter's father. What ensues is violent and unsettling.

Death Carries a Cane (*Passi di Danza su una Lama di Rasoio*, 1972), directed by Maurizio Pradeaux

The Italian title of this one translates as 'Dance Steps on the Edge of a Razor', which is actually a better title than the one that its English and American producers chose to go with. Such thoughts notwithstanding, this is still great fun for those who admire the genre, a film in which a variety of larger than life figures (with performances pitched at nigh-operatic levels) engage in plot and counterplot, with bloody murder the order of the day. Plotting is not the strong suit of Pradeaux's movie (but how often is it in *gialli*?), but the director is able to deliver the requisite nudity and mayhem with enough energy to make us forgive the rudimentary plotting and characterisation. In the final analysis, this is a film for *giallo* aficionados only, not for anyone looking to be converted – the latter will probably find the proceedings both dull and irritating.

Death Laid an Egg (*La Morte Ha Fatto l'Uovo*, 1967), directed by Giulio Questi

This brittle and effective film (one that has a substantial following) gives the appearance of an art movie as much as it does a *giallo*. Having said that, all the fingerprints of the genre are clearly in place, even when the director appears to be making salient points about the bourgeoisie and the hypocrisy of their lives. The film starts in a roadside hotel, where we see a variety of their guests engaged in bizarre pursuits: one man is on the point of committing suicide while another eavesdrops on a couple busy having sex in the next room. As this auditory voyeur climbs on to a balcony in order to see the sexual activity better, he sees a woman being savagely killed by a murderer wearing black gloves (what else? – it is a *giallo* after all). The killer turns out to be the owner of a chicken farm (shades of the equally dotty *Motel Hell*), and the subsequent outlandish plot includes details such as a scientist attempting to create headless, wingless chickens to maximise profits.

Don't Torture a Duckling (*Non Si Sevezia un Paperino*, 1972), directed by Lucio Fulci

If you think that this film has one of the oddest titles in a genre noted for such things, just a few frames of Lucio Fulci's film will convey the fact that it is barely surrealistic enough for this wildly over-plotted tale. In a town by a southern Italian mountain, young boys are being viciously killed. A local witch is encountered digging up the skeleton of a child and doing other suspicious things, but disapproval also falls on the mentally subnormal Giuseppe. A Milanese newsman is stirred into the brew and refuses to accept the suspicions of the townspeople. He interviews the priest of the town (notable for his stiff-necked religious rectitude) and Patricia, a seductive woman struggling with drugs. The revelation of the killer is hardly a piece of rocket science, but, along the way, Fulci delivers a variety of gruesome set pieces that have acquired a keen following for the film.

The Forbidden Photos of a Lady Above Suspicion (*Le Foto Proibite di una Signora per Bene*, 1970), directed by Luciano Ercoli

Ercoli was an inconsistent director, but this is one of his more notable efforts, furnished with one of Morricone's most impressive piano scores. If Dagmar Lassander's beleaguered heroine is a little underdeveloped, her ordeals are handled with great gusto, and her performance is counterbalanced by the more erotic and sexually ambiguous woman played by the director's wife Susan Scott. A striking young woman finds herself followed by a shadowy figure on the beach. After fetishistic and menacing games with a knife, he tells her that her husband has committed murder. As so often in the field, fetishistic imagery is the order of the day here, and those looking for a more enlightened feminist view of female sexuality should look elsewhere (in fact, it would probably be a good idea for such people to totally ignore the *giallo* genre altogether). But for those prepared to take the controversial fare on offer here without being disturbed, Ercoli delivers a feast of unsettling and erotic imagery.

Four Flies on Grey Velvet (*Quattro Mosche di Velluto Grigio*, 1971), directed by Dario Argento

Rock drummer Roberto, played by the American actor Michael Brandon, is stalked by a mysterious figure, who he then follows into what he thinks is an empty theatre. Roberto finds himself engaged in a fight, and stabs the assailant with his own knife. While this is happening, a masked figure has photographed the struggle, and Roberto is the victim of what appears to be a blackmailing scheme. All, of course, is not as it seems, and the murder in the theatre may not have happened at all. This was Argento's third film in the genre, and it is clear that he was beginning to spread his wings in terms of reinventing a genre that had already calcified into cliché. The main problem with the film is the uninspiring performance by Michael Brandon, delivering far less in the way of intriguing torment than (for instance) David Hemmings in *Deep Red* or other more charismatic male leads. Similarly, Mimsy Farmer as the female lead delivers a standard performance that doesn't make much of a mark. But many of the Argento visual trademark flourishes are firmly in place, and the film remains essential viewing for those interested in the development of the director's technique.

The Iguana with a Tongue of Fire (*L'Iguana dalla Lingua di Fuoco*, 1971), directed by Riccardo Freda

The fact that one of the most distinguished names in Italian genre cinema, the great Riccardo Freda, chose to direct this under the pseudonym of Willy Pareto speaks volumes about his own feelings. It is surprising that he should feel none too proud of this, given that other films on his CV (one would have thought) might have inspired a similar wish to disown them. In fact, the real reason why Freda may not be proud of this one is not so much its level of violence (no more or less than the average *giallo*) but its level of achievement: the director's visual flourishes are severely restrained compared with his customary standards. The credits sequence establishes that this is Dublin (*gialli* are never afraid to transplant their extremely Italianate actors into highly unlikely foreign cities). Soon after the opening sequence, an attractive young woman opens a door. A nameless assailant throws vitriol in her face, scarring her hideously, then raggedly opens her throat with a cut-throat razor. This extremely grisly beginning suggests that what follows will be a catalogue of horrors, but in fact such moments become rarer as the film progresses, although Freda pulls out all the stops for the eye-opening finale. Diplomatic immunity is stifling the investigation, so Inspector John Norton is brought in, a Dirty Harry-type who is prepared to bend the rules. The casting of this very Celtic copper is particularly unlikely, as Italian genre regular Luigi Pistilli plays the part; given his Italianate features and familiarity from other films in the genre, the accent he is saddled with seems even more unlikely than ever. As usual, a variety of red herrings are paraded before us, but it is clear that Freda was less than fully engaged with this material, until, that is, a mother and daughter (the latter in a state of Lolita-like undress) are menaced by a sexually ambiguous psychopath. As Norton bursts in and a bloody fight ensues, the entire scene reaches a level of delirium (and brutality – note the treatment of Norton's mother) that is unusual even in this genre. Nevertheless, *The Iguana* is very much a footnote in Freda's otherwise distinguished career.

A Lizard in a Woman's Skin (*Una Lucertola con la Pelle di Donna*, 1971), directed by Lucio Fulci

For many years, Fulci's seminal *giallo* was unavailable; recently audiences have been able to see it in a print that does more justice to his vision, but things are complicated: only a panned and scanned Italian-language print contains the uncensored cut (the language, with subtitles, isn't a problem, but the panning and scanning is), while the restored, surround-sound English-language print looks and sounds wonderful. The attraction of the latter, of course, is that so many of the actors in the cast are performing in English, with their own voices, notably Stanley Baker. This was one of the British actor's last films, and his performance shows just what a major presence he was in British cinema. In fact, his part (a police inspector suspicious of a society woman's involvement in the murder of her decadent neighbour) is nothing to write home about, being somewhat underwritten (Fulci and co-writer Roberto Gianviti characterised the detective only in terms of the tuneless whistle he is prone to). Baker's mere presence fills out the role admirably, as does another reliable British actor, Leo Genn, as the father of Florinda Bolkan, the woman under suspicion. Bolkan is, of course, an iconic figure in the genre, and delivers one of her most impressive performances as a woman suffering from strange, surrealistic dreams in which she appears to bloodily murder her neighbour after lesbian advances (to which she initially does not seem averse). This is the film that caused something of a sensation in Italy, involving a court case in which Fulci was accused of cruelty to animals. At one point (in one of her nightmares), Bolkan stumbles into a hospital laboratory where eviscerated dogs are stretched out on racks, their pulsing hearts and other organs clearly visible while receptacles catch their dripping blood. Amazingly, it was felt that these (to modern eyes) fairly obvious Rambaldi models were the real thing, and technicians had to produce the special effects in an Italian court to prove that real dogs had not been subjected to cruel treatment! The otherwise splendid-looking English-language print does not have this most famous sequence, and all the violence and nudity is trimmed (in the English-language print, Bolkan appears to be dressed when she commits the murders; the Italian print makes it clear that she, like her victim, is nude).

The New York Ripper (*Lo Squartatore di New York*, 1982), directed by Lucio Fulci

This is, of course, the Fulci film about which it is impossible to be objective. Either you will accept it as a typically over-the-top Fulci exercise in audience manipulation, or you will regard it as a piece of misogynistic trash, with the most graphic murders ever committed to film. If your objection is an ideological one, then there is nothing more to be said. But for those interested in the director's career, it remains a fascinating (if slightly reprehensible) work. The eviscerated body of a model is found in New York, and a woman on a bicycle is threatened by a figure simulating odd duck noises. Shortly afterwards, in a sex show, a female performer is grotesquely murdered with a bottle to the crotch. As the preceding makes clear, this is unrelenting stuff, and subsequent mutilations leave absolutely nothing to the imagination. But somewhat more disturbing is the director's truly jaundiced vision, and his lack of any truly sympathetic characters. The English actor Jack Hedley is cast as the investigating cop (and saddled with a crassly dubbed American accent), but for audiences who are prepared to test their limits in a kind of filmic equivalent of a rollercoaster ride, there is a case to be made for the film. Ironically, the one real miscalculation of the film is not to do with the bloodletting but with the odd decision to give the killer a duck-like voice. Why did Fulci think this would be an unsettling idea?

The Italian Western: Sergio Leone and Sergio Corbucci

Sergio Leone

For many years, it was generally considered that the greatest American westerns were those directed by John Ford and Howard Hawks. Both men were film-makers of immense vision, and their versions of the West are imbued with the strongest mythic underpinnings. In recent years, a certain shift in attitude towards these twin greats has been noted, as Ford's sentimentality has fallen out of favour, and the tough, psychologically complex westerns of Anthony Mann have come to be seen as the equals of Ford and Hawks. None of these American directors, however, portrayed anything that resembled the real West, the grimy, dirt-poor and visually unprepossessing country that we see in contemporary photographs.

When the westerns of Sergio Leone began to make their mark, several things happened simultaneously: Clint Eastwood, formerly the second-string star of a long-running TV western soap, *Raw Hide*, became a major international star; the violence of the Italian western – quickly, and disparagingly, described as spaghetti westerns – became the norm in the genre, and altered forever the face of the American western; and, most significantly of all, audiences had the impression that they were being presented with something closer to the real West. Clint Eastwood's character, with his dusty poncho, unshaven appearance and generally shop-worn demeanour, was a million miles away from the clean-cut, clean-shaven heroes of the great American westerns, and the supporting casts in these films have an almost operatic uncouthness.

Looked at in the twenty-first century, the great Italian westerns of Sergio Leone (and those of such contemporaries as Sergio Corbucci) now appear to be as far from the real West as the clean linen of their American predecessors. Firstly, the gunplay has an almost comic strip fantasy (American stars may have been unfeasibly quick on the draw, but could not shoot three men in a nanosecond, as Clint Eastwood appears to do in *A Fistful of Dollars* [*Un Pugno di Dollari*, 1964]). But we can also now see that Leone's heightened, artificial style was closer to the operas of Puccini than the westerns of John Ford, not least as the astonishing and eccentric scores of Ennio Morricone emphasised this unreal and subverted aspect of the Italian western.

Leone's first western, *A Fistful of Dollars*, was designed as the first instalment of a triptych. Leone had greatly admired the Kurosawa film *Yojimbo*, and had been fully aware that Kurosawa had lifted the central theme (a mercenary who plays two corrupt gangs off against each other). Why then should Leone himself not perform a similar act of homage? (In fact, the theme was to see considerably more service, notably in Walter Hill's riff on the idea in *Last Man Standing*.) Taking its theme from hardboiled Americana and relocating it into the context of a samurai tale had worked well; Leone clearly reasoned that the theme might function even better transposed back to the West, albeit set in a considerably earlier era than Hammett's *Red Harvest*.

Leone had noted the similarities between the film's theme and *commedia dell'arte*, along with the work of Goldoni (in particular *The Servant of Two Masters*). It is a notably male universe: where women feature significantly in the films of Ford, Hawks and Anthony Mann, Leone (at least until the appearance of the Claudia Cardinale figure in *Once Upon a Time in the West*) was more interested in exploring relationships between men – friendship, rivalry, etc – but without necessarily touching on any homoerotic themes.

For a Few Dollars More (*Per Qualche Dollaro in Più*, 1965) introduced another actor from the gallery of American character players – the gimlet-eyed Lee Van Cleef, perfectly cast as an ex-military man turned bounty hunter. Despite the fact that two Americans were now performing for Leone in English (a language the director only ever had a cursory understanding of), the film still seemed very much a product of Italy, even though such players as Gian Maria Volonte were, of course, dubbed. The success of both films was astonishing, and prepared the way for an American career for Eastwood (later to appear with equal success in a variety of sequels, *Dirty Harry* and a variety of American westerns that echoed his work with Leone, even down to the soundtracks: the score for *Hang' Em High* by Dominic Frontière is very much in the Morricone mould, with sudden dramatic shifts of emphasis and a notable foregrounding in the context of the action, much as Leone had utilised the music of Morricone in his films – Eastwood and Don Siegel, in fact, used the Italian maestro himself in their less than successful *Two Mules for Sister Sara*). Eastwood's 'Man with No Name' was one of the key creations of 1960s Italian cinema, and audiences had begun to anticipate the next Leone film with keen interest. Gone were the days when Leone had been obliged to masquerade under an American pseudonym to deceive both American and Italian audiences into thinking they were watching an American film, an indignity Mario Bava himself had suffered in his *gialli* and horror films.

The final film in the Dollars trilogy demonstrated, with its massive ambition and sheer length, that Leone was becoming interested in making films only on the grandest possible scale. *The Good, the Bad and the Ugly* (*Il Buono, il Brutto, il Cattivo*, 1966) both introduced an epic background (including a massively staged military battle) as a backdrop for its games of lethal one-upmanship between the protagonists (Eastwood and Van Cleef, the latter playing a different character) and the addition of a comic figure (Il Brutto), Eli Wallach. But a new level of sophistication was creeping into the director's otherwise mythic constructions. Who were the Good, the Bad and the Ugly of this film? While an easy answer suggests itself (Eastwood, Van Cleef and Wallach), the studied avoidance of the moral certainties of the American western made such conclusions far from straightforward. By placing his characters in the middle of a civil war, the exigencies of morality become even more tenuous.

After the success of *The Good, the Bad and the Ugly* (recently restored to the director's original vision, with an elderly Clint Eastwood and Eli Wallach voicing their younger selves in unused footage), Leone planned to shoot his ambitious gangster epic *Once Upon a Time in America* in the States, but found that the success of the westerns forced him to continue to mine this vein for some time yet. This was not entirely uncongenial to the director, who felt that he still had things to say in the medium, and proceeded to produce his masterpiece in the genre, *Once Upon a Time in the West* (*C'era una Volta il West*, 1968). While at the centre of this sprawling narrative was a revenge theme (involving the harmonica-playing Charles Bronson and the ruthless killer Henry Fonda, cast knowingly against type by Leone), the political and sociological implications of this very lengthy movie represented a new level of achievement on the part of the director. The iconic use of a woman in the film (played by the bewitching Claudia Cardinale, formerly a muse for another operatic Italian director, Fellini) also broadened his achievement. And Leone's confidence with the medium even extended to a lengthy sequence early in the movie (utilising such familiar genre faces as American character actors Jack Elam and Woody Stroud) which perfectly meshed with the more serious themes of expansionism and the growth of civilised society in the West that the film addressed.

Visually, Leone's films had always demonstrated the most impressive *mise-en-scène*, with the framing of his action illustrating a level of achievement rarely seen in the cinema before. *Once Upon a Time in the West* stripmined these elements of the director's skill, and another distinctive score by Morricone set the seal on the director's success.

But a first faltering was just around the corner, when Leone began *A Fistful of Dynamite* (also known as *Once Upon a Time… The Revolution*, or *Duck, You Sucker!* [*Giù la Testa*, 1971]). Here the heroic/comic duo was incarnated by James Coburn and Rod Steiger as an ex-IRA explosives expert and Mexican bandit. Leaving aside the film's unsophisticated treatment of Coburn's IRA past (par for the course, in any case, in Italian cinemas, which treated the Troubles with a romanticism that suggested it was a mere continuation of the American revolutionary war), there was clear evidence that the director was beginning to repeat himself, and the freshness of the earlier movies was replaced by a by-the-numbers approach. Leone had suggested Sam Peckinpah as a director, but the film's backers insisted that Leone direct the film. The original choices were Jason Robards in the Steiger role and Malcolm McDowell (who Leone had seen in *If*) as Sean, the IRA bomb-man (Leone feeling that the men of the IRA were young). The contracts, however, had been signed, and Steiger and Coburn were onboard. There was a clash of personality between Steiger and Leone, with the former treating his part with the kind of method-based seriousness that was his speciality (Leone's approach could not have been further from some of the more actor-friendly directors Steiger had worked with; Hitchcock was the closest model for Leone, with actors being utilised in a plastic fashion as one more element in the total *gesamtkunstwerk*, or total work of art, that was Leone's model). Looking at the indifferent achievement of *A Fistful of Dynamite* today, it seems bizarre to consider that Leone was inspired by the novels of Joseph Conrad when making the film, setting an intellectual who has been involved in a revolution against an unsophisticated Mexican. But the Mexican revolution in the film is not treated with any sophistication, and Leone's attempts to maintain the mythic framework quickly evaporate. Leone was well aware of the 'Oirish' sentimentality of John Ford, but was not interested in replicating this with any similar treatment of Coburn's IRA bomber character, and a certain pessimism undercut those loose-limbed, comic moments. Leone pointed out that the pessimism in his films was due to the fact that he was a Roman, and noted that being a Roman and being Italian were two different things, the former being more fatalistic. This he ascribed to the final decay and fall of the Roman Empire, but it led throughout his life to a political pessimism with regard to his own country (it would be interesting to know what Leone, were he alive today, would make of the Silvio Berlusconi's Italy, with the country's president being arraigned on a variety of corruption charges and altering the law in order to avoid prosecution). But the final effect of his film is upbeat, as the director's humanism undercuts the basic fatalism.

Leone was well aware of his place in Italian cinema, and made a conscious decision to be a populist filmmaker. He saw his movies as fables, and noted that his friend and colleague Francesco Rosi, who directed only political films, enjoyed a limited audience, whereas he had the attention of spectators throughout the world. He had no time for specific political statements in his films, and preferred to concentrate on character, delineated through close-ups: no director before (and few since) had crammed movies with so many massive close-ups, with even shots of human eyes filling the screen. During the 58 films he had made as an assistant, he had noticed that the directors he had worked with had stuck to certain rules, and he decided to break these (or at least create rules of his own). He regarded close-ups in his films as expressions of emotion, and was conscious that this formalism drew attention to itself (notably via the specific punctuations of Morricone's scores). Flashbacks were also integral to Leone's universe, and these always functioned in a markedly Freudian way. Leone was also well aware that his films were considered overlong by distributors, and it is a measure of his integrity that he simply refused to cut them (the corollary, of course, was that his films were often shown in mutilated forms that caused him great pain). The visual elements of the films were often inspired by fine art, with Goya's Disasters of War being utilised by the director as a paradigm. And for *Once Upon a Time in the West*, Leone introduced his director of photography, Tonino delli Colli, to a sequence of Rembrandt prints, and the director suggested that he wanted the monochromatic qualities of the Dutch master.

Leone was, of course, fully aware of the importance of Morricone's music in his films, but would not have been phased by the chuckles of amusement that the often tongue-in-cheek scoring created in British and American audiences in the early days of Italian westerns before Morricone's music achieved the popularity it subsequently obtained. He considered that the image of Italy as a nation of music lovers was entirely false, and noted that only three per cent of Italians listened to classical music (interestingly enough, those statistics are valid for both Britain and America, even in the twenty-first century). Leone was bemused by the fact that Stanley Kubrick had spoken to him and the only music of Ennio Morricone that he enjoyed was the work that he had done with Leone. Leone's explanation for this was the intensely personal nature of their collaboration; he was well aware that Morricone was able to turn out music by the numbers for other directors, a syndrome that simply didn't exist in the Leone/Morricone collaboration.

His last film, *Once Upon a Time in America*, is outside the scope of this book, but remains a remarkable coda to a remarkable career.

Sergio Corbucci

The story of Sergio Leone, of course, is by no means the only index to the Italian western, which during its time of greatest popularity produced hundreds of films of varying quality. Other directors, such as Sergio Corbucci, produced work of great interest and accomplishment (see the separate note on Corbucci's *Django*) and several other Italian western directors took on themes of political significance. Corbucci, who was born in 1926 in Rome and died there in 1990, also worked under unlikely pseudonyms such as Gordon Wilson Jr and Stanley Corbet. Like Leone, he was prepared to tackle (and make a success of) a variety of disparate genres. But few would deny that (again like the other Sergio) his metier was the western. Corbucci was another director, like Lindsay Anderson in the UK and François Truffaut in France, who began his career as a writer on film, a career trajectory also embraced by Dario Argento and other Italian talents. His first work was as assistant director to Robert Rossellini, before he began his own directing career in the 1950s. As with so many Italian directors, he was obliged to turn his hand to whatever genres were available, from unsophisticated comedies with popular star Totò to a variety of *pepla*. His early contact with the other Sergio (Leone) on *The Slave* (1962) was a demonstration of the common territory of the two men.

When Corbucci began directing westerns (as did so many of his contemporaries), it was quickly apparent that he was a considerable talent. While less innovative than Leone, his greater number of movies shows, perhaps, a slightly broader universe, and his westerns were able to take onboard both parody and politics with panache. His best known film (and the only other Italian western to match Leone's in popularity) was, of course, 1966's *Django* (see separate section), and the film defined the Italian western quite as much as the Dollars trilogy. Looked at today, for all its energy and invention, it does not possess the more sophisticated elements of political thought to be found in Corbucci's later films, such as the remarkable *Great Silence* (*Il Grande Silenzio*, 1968). This unusual piece was notable for the bleakness of its snow-bound locales, and demonstrated the anti-establishment stance that was to be a hallmark of his later work.

A mini-series of films that Corbucci initiated was described by the director himself as 'proletarian fables', which posited an antithesis between socialism and capitalism in the form of a Mexican revolutionary and an American adventurer. *The Mercenary* (*Il Mercenario*), also known as *A Professional Gun*, is the first significant entry in this series. Many consider this to be (along with 1970's *Companeros*) Corbucci's most accomplished film. Despite some ill-advised humour (such as the angelic costumes sported by the revolutionaries), the film has many virtues. Tony Musante, as the energetic rebel, turns in a performance quite as interesting as the one he gave for Dario Argento in *The Bird with the Crystal Plumage* (*L'Uccello dalle Piume di Cristallo*) and genre stalwart Franco Nero is as reliable as ever as the mercenary who joins forces with him. Anyone who has seen the film remembers Jack Palance's flamboyant gay gunman and the blood-boltered demise of his character in the middle of a circus ring. But a measure of the film's accomplishment is its dialectic of revolution, as discussed by Musante and Nero, along with the variety of character shifts in the film. The cinematography has a raw energy that is characteristic of Corbucci's films.

There are those who regard *Companeros* (1970) as the director's most interesting film (certainly it is impossible to forget the title after a few bars of Ennio Morricone's naggingly ingratiating coral theme). The cast is a showcase of the international actors (European and American) who by now were attracted to the genre: Tomas Milian, the inevitable Franco Nero, Fernando Rey (who had appeared in Bunuel's films), Karin Schubert and, again, Jack Palance. The film demonstrates how thoroughly Corbucci embraced France Nero as 'his' actor (much in the way that Anthony Mann's best films were made with James Stewart and Leone's with Clint Eastwood), and Nero's performance, balancing wryness and cynicism, is perfectly judged. Opinions on Jack Palance's operatic performance are divided. Despite his obvious skills, Palance (like Rod Steiger) was an actor who needed discipline from his director, and clearly not much was on offer from Corbucci in *Companeros*. But given that his character possesses a wooden hand (having once been nailed to a cross and freed when his tame hawk chewed away his hand), it is apparent that Ingmar Bergman-style subtlety would not have been appropriate to the character. But underneath the tongue-in-cheek elements of the film, there is still the same rigour that distinguishes the director's other films. Tomas Milian, as the revolutionary, affects Che Guevara-style dress, and joins forces with Nero to liberate a professor (played by Fernando Rey) and his students. It goes without saying that a certain indulgence of the sardonic approach of the film is necessary, but for those viewers able to get beyond this, there are rewards here. Regrettably, this approach to humour was to become broader and broader with the slapstick westerns staring Terence Hill and Bud Spencer. Other westerns directed by Corbucci include 1964's *Minnesota Clay*, *Ringo and His Golden Pistol* (*Johnny Oro*) in 1966, and *Navajo Joe* (*Un Dollaro a Testa*), also in 1966.

Along with Leone's *Dollars* trilogy, the operatically violent *Django* (1966) is the most influential of all spaghetti westerns, a genuinely iconic movie that (as with Leone in *A Fistful of Dollars*) plunders Kurosawa's *Yojimbo* for its plot (a man of violence, servant of two corrupt masters, plays both against each other, assuring their destruction – a plot, in fact, that Kurosawa himself had lifted from Dashiell Hammett's *Red Harvest*). Originally banned in several countries for its then-extreme violence (and denied a certificate by the BBFC in the UK until 1993), the film made a star of Franco Nero and spawned over 30 unauthorised sequels.

It is, of course, the extreme violence that earned the film its reputation: a corrupt preacher, who spies for the villainous Major Jackson, has an ear bloodily cut off – a scene referenced in Quentin Tarantino's *Reservoir Dogs* – and then is fed the severed organ; Django himself undergoes the kind of sadomasochistic violence that Brando made such a key ingredient of his screen persona, notably having his hands broken and turned into bloody messes by a Mexican's rifle butt and horse's hooves (the significance of the mutilation of Django's hands is somewhat undercut by the speedy dispatch of six heavies in the final scene – realism isn't the order of the day here).

But it's Corbucci's dynamic eye for a composition that marks the film out as something quite new in the western – along with Leone, the director (like his friend, a veteran of a previous Italian trend, the muscleman *peplum*) inaugurates a muddy, dirty vision of the West which (for all its implausible gunplay) looks more like the real thing than any Hollywood westerns of the classic era; the unprepossessing prostitutes in *Django*, for instance, are a million miles away from the lacquered Linda Darnell in Ford's *My Darling Clementine*. And his kinetic grasp of the language of cinema makes *Django* as vigorous an experience as anything the Italian cinema had produced.

Much was made at the time (and subsequently) of the Italian western's creation of a new, hyper-cynical protagonist: the mercenary out only for himself (with a residual regard for the poor and the brutalised; women are the recipients of rough gallantry from both Django and Leone's Man with No Name). But if the truth were told, the truly cynical western hero was not an Italian invention – the disillusioned anti-heroes of the series of ambitious westerns Anthony Mann made with James Stewart are far richer and more nuanced creations than anything Corbucci and co. created, with psychological depths and conflicts the Italian directors were clearly uninterested in. Django's motivation (beyond revenge for a dead woman) as he cuts a swathe through the racist thugs of Major Jackson and the sadistic brutality of the Mexican rebels is strictly one dimensional. But there is no point in criticising Corbucci for what he didn't try to do – his achievement, even viewed after the Italian westerns vanished beneath a slew of ever-more-spiritless clones, remains both iconoclastic and trenchant.

Italian Cinema: The Films

1900 (*Novecento*, 1976), directed by Bernardo Bertolucci

Bertolucci's attraction to the epic is matched by his fondness for epochal events. Recently this has seen a diverting, if slight, expression in *The Dreamers*, but here key events in Italian history are perceived through the eyes of Alfredo (Robert De Niro) and Olmo (Gérard Depardieu), both born in January 1901, following their lives until the Liberation in 1945. The two men come from vastly different social backgrounds (the peasantry and the aristocracy) and Alfredo, whose father is the lord of the manor, is the one least able to deal with the social differences between him and his friend. His father is played by Burt Lancaster, giving the kind of performance he had honed for Visconti. Music is used in a foregrounded fashion here (the score is by Ennio Morricone) and specifically the music of Verdi is utilised emblematically. While the wildly multinational casting generally works well, it is a shame that Donald Sutherland, as a petty Fascist, is encouraged to turn in a one-note performance, almost as if Bertolucci does not trust his audience's intelligence in responding to the character. Nevertheless, the achievement of the film is considerable, with the visuals often truly breathtaking.

Africa Addio (1965), directed by Gualtiero Jacopetti

The *Mondo Cane* school of documentary-making was at one time phenomenally successful across the world, but later degenerated into such (largely faked) atrocity catalogues that were the hallmark of the *Faces of Death* films. This one is directed by Jacopetti, father of the genre, and thus deserves consideration, although it's clear that he was by this point running out of steam, even though the copious scenes of animal slaughter, live executions and grisly tribal rituals provided as much material as ever. As always, the attempt at a balanced, scholarly tone is somewhat undercut by the relish of the filmmakers for the material (although audiences still clearly shared this relish).

Allegro Non Troppo (1976), directed by Bruno Bozzetto

When the Disney organisation belatedly made a sequel to its phenomenally successful *Fantasia*, they had in fact already been beaten to the punch. Disney's bold attempt to marry state-of-the-art cartoon imagery with several sequences of much-loved classical music was a signature film in introducing music to generation after generation. But before Disney's sequel, Bozzetto had made this imaginative and stimulating entry, utilising music by Debussy, Ravel, Sibelius, Dvorak and Stravinsky. For all the virtues of Bozzetto's film, there are several severe miscalculations, such as the ill-advised live action scenes, which are desperately unamusing. Similarly, the sequences animated to the music of Sibelius et al are inconsistent, but there is enough imagination on view to ensure that the marriage is a happy one. And when the visual imagination on the screen falters, there's always that glorious music...

Amici per la Pelle (*Friends for Life*, 1955), directed by Franco Rossi

Several directors have made a virtue of achieving truthful, unsentimental portrayals from child actors, notably Philip Leacock in the UK and Steven Spielberg in the USA. If the latter at times seems to be tempted by sentimentality he should perhaps look at Rossi's remarkable film, which has two of the best performances by children in any movie. A schoolboy finds himself staying with the family of a friend, and becomes aware that life can be very different from that of his own unhappy home (his mother is dead). The two young friends have a disagreement, and the boy joins his father on a business trip to the Middle East, with unhappy results for both friends. The director's observation of the rites and rules of childhood is handled with rigour and a clear-eyed view of the way human beings (of whatever age) behave towards each other.

The Arabian Nights (*Il Fiore delle Mille e Una Notti*, 1974), directed by Pier Paolo Pasolini

Pasolini's erotic trilogy (this film and 1971's *The Decameron*, along with the following year's *The Canterbury Tales*) created something of a censorship stir in its day, with the earthiness of the sexual depictions (including the odd erection). Today, of course, they would hardly raise an eyebrow and time has, generally, been kind to them, even though Pasolini's use of non-actors achieved (as always in such cases) mixed results. The ten tales from *A 1,001 Nights* were handled with real brio by the director, whose celebration of heterosexual love is not at all compromised by his own gay leanings. While the non-professional actors often find the demands of their roles beyond their limited abilities, an undoubted earthiness is conveyed by the use of such a cast, and the settings (including Iran and Yemen) are stark and beautiful. Looked at today, the trilogy has much to offer, alongside its occasional clumsiness and longueurs. Shot in the exotic settings of Ethiopia, Yemen, Nepal and Iran, *The Arabian Nights* celebrates guiltless, heterosexual love within a universe of magical signs and evil jinns who are all subject to the vagaries of destiny. Ennio Morricone contributes beautiful, sparse musical motifs.

L'Assassino (*The Assassin*, 1961), directed by Elio Petri

Petri and Marcello Mastroianni enjoyed a successful

collaboration, and the director's debut film shows a talent that already has much to offer. An antique dealer finds himself accused of murder, even though he is innocent. Mastroianni's performance is subtle and allusive, conveying the conflicted personality of his protagonist with the actor's customary skill. Petri is particularly good at building up the variety of vague threats to the equilibrium of his beleaguered hero.

The Bandits at Orgosolo (*I Banditi a Orgosolo*, 1961), directed by Vittorio De Seta

This 1961 film was an important later off-shoot of the Neorealist movement, with its cast of Sardinian peasants ably handled by De Seta, whose previous experience had been in documentary films. When a young shepherd finds himself accused of a crime he did not commit, he escapes, taking his sheep with him. The death of the sheep alters his destiny, however, rather in the fashion that a similar catastrophe changes the life of Gabriel Oak in Thomas Hardy's *Far From the Madding Crowd*. The film enjoyed a wide audience outside Italy.

The Battle of Algiers (*La Battaglia di Algeri*, 1965), directed by Gillo Pontecorvo

Over the years, the reputation of Pontecorvo's powerful and gritty documentary-style film has grown, helped not a little by the fame of Ennio Morricone's groundbreaking score. The radical approach of the film was to show the Algerian movement for independence from the point of view of the participants, shooting in the actual locales where the events took place. No newsreel footage is utilised in the film, but its documentary air is persuasive indeed. For many years the film was banned in France, but it is not simplistic in the conclusions it draws about the conflict. Pontecorvo's film won the best film award at the Venice Film Festival in 1966.

Before the Revolution (*Prima della Rivoluzione*, 1964), directed by Bernardo Bertolucci

This is one of the films with which Bertolucci initially made his mark as a director, and, in the light of recent works such as *Little Buddha*, it now seems very much part of a golden age for the director. Francesco Barilli plays a young man from a middle-class background living in Parma. While his lifestyle is the epitome of bourgeois steadiness, he is drawn to radical politics. Similarly, he is obliged to choose between a conventional marriage and a more sensuous affair with a young relative played by Adriana Asti. Bertolucci's achievement here is highly impressive, with the various choices for his protagonist laid out intelligently. If there is a fault, it is the self-conscious, referential use of ideas from Marx and Freud.

The Canterbury Tales (*I Racconti di Canterbury*, 1971), directed by Pier Paolo Pasolini

Pasolini's 1971 attempt at filming a classic English author (who was himself influenced, of course, by *The*

Decameron, which Pasolini had already filmed in the same year) is a mixed success, and in some ways a very strange film indeed. Plunging with gusto into some of the blackest and bawdiest of the tales, Pasolini celebrates almost every conceivable form of sexual act with a rich, earthy humour and weaves a visual magic which draws on the work of artists such as Bruegel and Bosch. Pasolini himself takes the part of Chaucer. One might have thought that the presence of English actors such as Hugh Griffith and Tom Baker in the film might have the effect of anglicising it, but as they are cast alongside Laura Betti and Pasolini regular Franco Citti, the final effect suggests some strange alternate universe which has little to do with Chaucer (or even Italy, for that matter). As always in Pasolini's erratic trilogy, comic invention is always to be found, along with enthusiastic sexuality. If some of the performances seem strained, that is perhaps understandable; less acceptable are the rather dull stretches that interleave what one might expect to be a constantly eye-opening experience.

Il Caso Mattei (*The Mattei Affair*, 1972), directed by Francesco Rosi and Tonino Guerra

The collaboration between Francesco Rosi and the actor Gian Maria Volonté is not as celebrated as, say, that of Max Von Sydow and Ingmar Bergman or Mastroianni and Fellini, but the results are often very impressive indeed. One of Rosi's most acclaimed films is this study of the life and death (in a plane crash) of the socialist oil tycoon Enrico Mattei. Utilising the naturalistic style of his early work, in some ways this is a Citizen Cane-like study of the corrupting influence of power, with Volonté fully up to the demands of his enigmatic role. The film won the best film award at Cannes in 1972.

Christ Stopped at Eboli (*Cristo si é Fermato a Eboli*, 1979), directed by Francesco Rosi

With a striking score by Piero Piccioni and a remarkable performance by Gian Maria Volonté as the writer Carlo Levi, Rosi's film is an outstanding achievement and a bold stab at Levi's famous book. When the protagonist is forced to flee to an almost medieval southern village when his anti-fascist views become unacceptable in Turin, he is required to make adjustments to his new surroundings. The mountain village and its inhabitants force him to consider afresh his attitude to his fellow countrymen. The incidental pleasures throughout the film are many, although it is Volonté's central performance that holds the eye. If the pace is a mite leisurely, patience is rewarded by Rosi's insights.

Cinema Paradiso (1988), directed by Giuseppe Tornatore

This story of a small boy whose father has been killed in the Second World War and finds a surrogate father in the local projectionist is one of the most popular and celebrated Italian films to achieve worldwide recognition in many years. For all its virtues, however, it remains a notably meretricious and manipulative piece of work: mawkish, artificial and lacking in any real truth (apart from incidental details). Its massive success is, of course, due to its 'cute' child protagonist. For all the trappings of realism for which the film received acclaim, the use of the youthful Salvatore Cascio is not a million miles away from the heart-tugging appeal of Shirley Temple in her now unwatchable Hollywood films. The ever reliable Philippe Noiret (dubbed here) occasionally manages to triumph over his material.

City of Women (*La Città delle Donne*, 1980), directed by Federico Fellini

What were Marcello Mastroianni and Federico Fellini thinking while they were making this film? The businessman who leaves a train to find himself in a society of women has many elements of the director and star's earlier work together, notably *8?*. The fact that all the things that make the earlier work great appear here as inept clichés surely must have occurred to them both, but did not provide the fresh injection of inspiration so sorely needed. There are good things here certainly (how can any film with this director and star be devoid of interest?), but there is none of the arresting cinematic flair of their earlier work together.

Il Conformista (*The Conformist*, 1969), directed by Bernardo Bertolucci

One of Bertolucci's most impressive films, with

galvanic performances from Jean-Louis Trintignant and Stefania Sandrelli. Bertolucci's anti-hero is a repressed homosexual who shot a man who attempted to molest him when he was a child. He decides to enter into a loveless marriage, and agrees to act for the Fascist party. His assignment is to kill his ex-professor. The synthesis of politics and Freudian psychology is fastidiously maintained, and the two female stars in particular (Sandrelli and Dominique Sanda) offer Bergmanesque performances.

Conversation Piece (*Gruppo di Famiglia in un Interno*, 1974), directed by Luchino Visconti

While the collaboration of director (Visconti) and star (Burt Lancaster) is successful in *Conversation Piece*, this is a much more restrained and less operatic work than *The Leopard*. A professor enjoys a quiet life surrounded by his collection of *objets d'art* in his Roman apartment. He is persuaded to rent a room to a countess (played by Silvana Mangano, so magnetic in earlier films for the director) and her innamorato, Helmut Berger. The effect of all this on the professor, who is fighting his own homosexual impulses, is significant. Visconti had not been in the best of health when he made this film, and this may account for why the drama is to some extent undernourished. But the expressive performances pay off, although the ill-judged comedy (in which bourgeois sensibilities are lampooned) seems desperately miscalculated.

Cronaca di una Morte Annunciata (*Chronicle of a Death Foretold*, 1987), directed by Francesco Rosi

A young man (played by Alain Delon) is killed after taking the virginity of a pretty young woman (Ornella Muti) and her marriage to a wealthy young man collapses. The scenario of Rosi's film involves the investigation by a doctor, Gian Maria Volonté (who ten years earlier had starred in the director's *Christ Stopped at Eboli*), and his version of Gabriel Garcia Marquez's celebrated novel manages to include many of the levels of meaning that were ingrained in the original book. As a comment on inflexible codes of behaviour, the film is cutting, although the final effect lacks the rigour of Rosi's best work.

Cronaca Familiare (*Family Diary*, 1962), directed by Valerio Zurlini

Valerio Zurlini's 1962 film has a stately pace that might be something of a shock to modern audiences (used to films designed for shorter attention spans) but more than repays close attention. Marcello Mastroianni plays Enrico, devastated when his younger brother dies from a fatal disease. Finding himself unable to work, he meditates on his brother's all too brief life, and the separations and reunions that the two of them experienced. Based on Vasco Pratolini's novel, this is a film of subtle and nuanced feeling, with Mastroianni demonstrating yet again his mastery of the most understated forms of screen acting. For those able to seek it out, the precise and detailed visual style, along with the superb performances, make it more than worthwhile.

Death in Venice (*Morte a Venezia*, 1971), directed by Luchino Visconti

The hypnotic effect of Visconti's version of Thomas Mann's novella was immeasurably enhanced by the use of the music of Mahler throughout, notably the adagietto from the composer's fifth symphony. This was facilitated by Visconti changing the profession of his repressed central figure from a writer to a composer, so that his futile pursuit of a beautiful young man in a plague-stricken Venice could be played to the plangent orchestrations of the great symphonist. It was this, as much as Bogarde's beautifully understated performance that made the film such a massive international success in its heyday, but the astonishing visuals remain as impressive as ever, as do such details as the fragile performance of Silvana Mangano as mother of the seductive boy Tadzio. Looked at today, the dialectical discussions between the composer and his associate (played by Mark Burns) wear less well, but the film is still a work of consummate craftsmanship.

Death Occurred Last Night (*La Morte Risale a Ieri Sera*, 1970), directed by Duccio Tessari

A young woman vanishes, and the police realise that their work is cut out for them when her father (Raf Vallone) tells them that she possesses a mental age of three, along with a predisposition to nymphomania. The hunt that ensues, led by Inspector Lambert (Frank Wolff), plunges the viewer into a seedy world of prostitution and vice. While initially Tessari's film may function on the level of a kind of thriller, his strip-mining of the societal values that created the world of his characters is acute and unforgiving.

The Decameron (*Il Decamerone*, 1971), directed by Pier Paolo Pasolini

The first of Pasolini's Trilogy of Life films based on famous story cycles contains ten stories based on the fourteenth century works of Giovanni Boccaccio. The film romps through these tales of sex and death, perfectly capturing the bawdy, earthy, anarchic comic spirit of the original, though compromised by the hit-or-miss performances of the non-professional cast.

Il Deserto Rosso (*The Red Desert*, 1964), directed by Michelangelo Antonioni

Monica Vitti plays an engineer's wife adrift in the stark industrial landscape of Northern Italy — she has a nervous breakdown, attempts suicide and starts a tentative affair. In this key work — and his first film in colour — Antonioni deploys colour to extraordinary emotional effect, suggesting the interior landscape of his main character by the non-realist colouring of the landscape around her. In his carefully framed compositions, objects resemble elements in an abstract painting, while

Vitti crumples fetchingly against decaying walls as jets roar overhead.

Divorce Italian Style (*Divorzio all'Italiana*, 1961), directed by Pietro Germi

This was the first of the Italian sex comedies of the 1960s that enjoyed considerable success abroad. Stalwarts of the genre, Marcello Mastroianni and Stefania Sandrelli, are present, moving effortlessly from their work in more sedate art films to the rumbustious comedy on offer here. What made the film rather daring in its day was its attack on Italian male values, as well as the outdated laws relating to divorce, which ruffled a few feathers at the time. Mastroianni's appearance in the film became very well known, with his oiled hair and Hercule Poirot-style moustache.

I Fidanzati (*The Engagement*, 1963), directed by Ermanno Olmi

A welding job in Sicily tempts the hero of Olmi's film from his betrothed in Milan. He is happy about the 18-month contract, considering that it will enrich the relationship. He is wrong: the loneliness begins to tell, and soon he is obliged to take some tough decisions. Olmi's use of non-professionals as his protagonists is largely successful, although neither Carlo Cabrini nor Anna Canzi is quite up to the more subtle demands of their roles. But the film's success in its day was partly due to the naturalistic shooting and use of locales (along with the non-professional actors), which firmly removed the film from any notions of a kind of Hollywood artificiality.

La Famiglia (*The Family*, 1987), directed by Ettore Scola

The ambition of Ettore Scola's film is considerable, following the life of a man from his birth to his 80th birthday, when several generations of his family celebrate the occasion. Vittorio Gassman gives a customarily expressive performance in the lead role, and his wistfulness about a love that might have been (to the beguiling Fanny Ardant) is handled elegantly. Scola's concern is not with society but with the individual, and that makes his examination of character here distinctive and powerful. As with so many Italian films, however, Scola is unable to maintain any semblance of concision, and the film outstays its welcome.

Fellini Satyricon (1969), directed by Federico Fellini

Fellini's film was one of the few 'art' films to get a major circuit release in 1969, no doubt due to its erotic content. The experience of watching such a surrealistic and visceral film must have been strange indeed for those regular habitués of the Odeon circuit, tempted in by the promise of naked male and female flesh (generously supplied by the director). Martin Potter and Hiram Keller play two students in Ancient Rome who begin the film with a squabble over an attractive young boy. They then find themselves in a series of orgies and other sexual escapades (along with a spell on a slave ship and an encounter with a mythological monster). Petronius's story is a mere springboard for the over-the-top imagination displayed by Fellini, and the Rome presented in the film is like no Rome that ever existed. In fact, the final effect is of a slightly lascivious science fiction film with a heaving and energetic tale of concupiscence among some strange alien race. As so often with later Fellini, structure is pretty well jettisoned in favour of a series of strikingly staged set pieces. On that level, of course, Fellini (as always) delivers.

The Four Days of Naples (*Le Quattro Giornate di Napoli*, 1962), directed by Nanni Loy

Highly celebrated in its day, Nanni Loy's film retains a grim power in the twenty-first century. The occupying German forces rounded up the Italian male population in 1943 and despatched them to camps, but violent resistance was mounted by the inhabitants of Naples, who managed to triumph over the Nazis. All of this is handled with a highly impressive, tragic force by Loy, and while the events pictured in the film are period-specific, its timeliness remains striking.

The Garden of the Finzi-Continis (*Il Giardino dei Finzi-Contini*, 1970), directed by Vittorio De Sica

The contrast between De Sica's early neorealist films

and the sumptuousness of this late work could not be more marked, and it is not all to the director's credit that the sometimes hypnotic surfaces vitiate the dramatic tension of the work. Nevertheless, this is one of the director's finest films, and its best foreign film Oscar in 1971 (and well as the Berlin Prize) correctly celebrate De Sica's return to form after several indifferent films. The Ferrara mansion is the home of the wealthy and sophisticated Finzi-Contini family, who are Jewish. The arrival of the Fascist forces soon creates in them a siege mentality, and family members Dominique Sanda and Lino Capolicchio decide to open their tennis courts when a Jewish ban is imposed at the local club. As a picture of human beings coming to terms with the unimaginable, the film is subtle and nuanced, with the director's powers of observation as sharp as ever. His sympathy for this cultivated family is of an order with that he showed towards the eponymous bicycle thief and his son, and as a picture of a subject that is still painful in Italy today (the country's collusion with the Nazis) the film remains forthright and powerful.

The Girl Friends (*Le Amiche*, 1955), directed by Michelangelo Antonioni

Eleanora Rossi Drago plays a young woman who has succeeded as a fashion designer in Rome, and takes a trip back to her home town of Turin, where she finds that four of her close friends are experiencing turbulent private lives. In 1955, this film drew attention to

Antonioni as one of the most promising directors in Italy, a promise he was (of course) subsequently to fulfil. The story (adapted from Cesare Pavese) features a large dramatis personae, all handled with sensitivity and fastidiousness. While Italian cinema was still in thrall to a working-class vision (even from predominantly middle-class directors), Antonioni already demonstrated that he was interested in dealing with his own class, never closing his eyes to their foibles but always retaining a sympathy, often held at an intelligent distance. What particularly distinguishes the film, as so often with the director, is his subtle and intelligent handling of actors, here the cast (Drago, Valentina Cortese, Gabriele Ferzetti and Yvonne Furneaux) turns in ensemble playing of a rare order.

The Golden Coach (*La Carrozza d'Oro*, 1952), directed by Jean Renoir

An intriguing crossbreed made by the great French director in Italy in 1952. Set in eigtheenth century Peru, the film centres on a peripatetic Commedia dell'Arte company that attracts the attention of a variety of characters, including a bullfighter played by Ricardo Rioli and a viceroy played by Duncan Lamont. The centre of the film is Anna Magnani, in a part that could have been better played by an actress of more ethereal appeal, such as Silvana Mangano. Nevertheless, the teeming, rumbustious existence of the troupe is played with the vividness one would expect from Renoir, and as a strange, multinational pot-pourri, the film is particularly effective. It is intriguing to note that later movies, involving actors and directors from a variety of countries, often had the effect of producing an indigestible 'Euro-pudding'. Not here, however.

The Gospel According to Saint Matthew (*Il Vangelo Secondo Matteo*, 1964), directed by Pier Paolo Pasolini

The classic Hollywood image of Christ is, of course, Jeffery Hunter in Nicholas Ray's *King of Kings*: distinctly Ayrian, blue-eyed and non-Semitic. Even a director as rebellious as Ray could not shake off the constraints involved in making a film of the life of Christ, but (long before Martin Scorsese) the left-wing and gay Pasolini produced one of the most powerful – and least sentimental – treatments of the story. The film is most famous for the Marxist beliefs of the director, and there is no question that the behaviour of Christ (played by Enrique Irazoqui) takes on elements of a critique of society – no dewy-eyed softness here, but a rigorous, energetic figure. The film is deliberately stripped down in its manner, as if in response to the inert splendour of most Hollywood biblical epics, although the film is not lacking in majesty, as Pasolini's use of composers such as Bach, Mozart and Prokofiev lend an air of grandeur. The fact that clerical money was involved in the making of the film may undercut its reputation as a non-believer's view of the Christ story, but certainly for those unpersuaded by religion it remains one of the few watchable religious movies.

Hands over the City (*Le Mani sulla Città*, 1963), directed by Francesco Rosi

The early 1960s was a golden age for Italian cinema, and Rosi's film (which won the best film award at Venice in 1963) is still as powerful as when it was made. What makes the director's achievement striking is a certain problem he set for himself. While utilising his customary cast of non-actors, Rosi also cast Rod Steiger as a political wheeler-dealer, and the contrast between one of the most stylised of American actors with non-professionals could have been a recipe for disaster. Rosi's achievement is to synthesise the two opposing styles at work here and to make his sociological document a unified whole. A building collapses in one of the impoverished parts of Naples, killing the inhabitants. This event is to have an important impact on the municipal local elections. As so often with Rosi, political corruption is the theme here, and the anger engendered in the director by his theme fairly leaps off the screen.

Identification of a Woman (*Identificazione di una Donna*, 1982), directed by Michelangelo Antonioni

Michelangelo Antonioni's later films (after the universal success his mid-period films enjoyed) are something of a mixed bag. But, of course, nothing Antonioni directed could be without interest, and such is the case with this 1982 drama. A film director (Tomas Milian) is looking for a woman for a forthcoming project. He finds himself alienated from his upper-crust girlfriend (Daniela Silverio) and begins a relationship with a young actress (played by Christine Boisson), only the solution to his personal and artistic problems does not lie with her. At the time he made *Identification of a Woman*, Antonioni had been working in video (with mixed results) and some of that new sensibility is to be found here. While the visual appeal of the film is as commanding as one might expect, there is a glacial quality to the proceedings that is rarely transcended (in the way that similarly cool surfaces concealed intense emotion in early films such as *L'Avventura*). Although the film evokes the director's earlier work, the effect is actually to remind one how much more assured such films as *La Notte* were. With the director back on the familiar turf of the perennial difficulty of relationships in the modern world, the customary beauty of his work is here overlaid with an overt eroticism as Antonioni's filmmaker hero entangles himself with two women.

L'Innocente (*The Innocent*, 1976), directed by Luchino Visconti

Luchino Visconti's final film, adapted from a book by Gabriele D'Annunzio, shows signs of the director's incapacity when he made it, but is still a highly impressive final testament of a lustrous career, crammed with civilised virtues. Giancarlo Giannini plays a man from a privileged background who allows his marriage to flounder when he finds himself attracted to a young woman (played by Jennifer O'Neill). His wife (Laura Antonelli) also decides on some extra-marital dalliance, but tragedy is in the offing for the couple. The period settings here are handled with the assurance that one, of course, looks forward to from the director, and the acting is generally of a standard that one expects (although Jennifer O'Neill is perhaps a shade uninvolved).

Investigation of a Citizen above Suspicion (*Indagine su un Cittadino al di Sopra di Ogni Sospetto*, 1970), directed by Elio Petri

Gian Maria Volonté gives one of his most striking performances in Petri's powerful film, which won the best foreign film Oscar in 1970 as well as the Cannes special jury prize in the same year. In a rigorous examination of the classic crime novel trope, a woman's throat is slashed and a variety of clues point to the murderer. But the killer is in fact a Roman policeman who is intrigued to see whether his colleagues will be able to identify him as the murderer (he is, after all, a citizen 'above suspicion'). The director's left-wing sympathies upset the Right when the film appeared, which undoubtedly added to the film's fame. But while the direction is frequently over-emphatic, Volonté's charismatic performance as the murderer makes for a commanding cinematic experience.

Mamma Roma (1962), directed by Pier Paolo Pasolini

Pier Paolo Pasolini kept faith with his favoured low-life settings in his second film, which features Anna Magnani (the Mamma Roma of the title) in another powerhouse performance as a prostitute attempting to change her life by moving to a new part of town. One of Pasolini's more realist films, its mood is convincingly sombre.

Man of Straw (*L'Uomo di Paglia*, 1958), directed by Pietro Germi

In Germi's accessible and incisive film, a marriage is put under strain when the husband (Pietro Germi himself) has an affair with a younger woman (Franca Bettoja). In particular, his relationship with his youthful son suffers, and in many ways this is the crux of the film. Germi is particularly sharp on the hopefulness with which human beings approach what, in their hearts, they know to be hopeless situations, but audiences who might have expected to be able to second-guess the narrative here were surprised by the developments of the plot. This brilliantly written study of adultery is handled by the director in a dispassionate but involving fashion, and what makes the film function particularly powerfully is the assured performances he obtains from his cast.

Medea (1969), directed by Pier Paolo Pasolini

Pasolini's 1969 film of the Euripides tragedy is not held in particularly high esteem these days, although it is a creditable stab by a director fully in sympathy with his material. Two cultures clash when Medea, the 'barbarian princess', is brought home to secular Corinth by her lover Jason. Maria Callas is extraordinary as Medea in Pasolini's reworked version of Euripides' drama, told in majestic cinematic tableaux with a spectacular array of gorgeously costumed figures. Ironically, the casting of Maria Callas in a non-singing role as Medea was, at the time, considered to be the film's trump card – surely the singer's undoubted dramatic skills would translate effectively into the new medium? In the final analysis, Callas, deprived of the greatest weapon in her armoury (her singing voice), did not plumb the tragic depths of the part, although her performance, like the film itself, looked good, with Ennio Guarnieri's cinematography adding a lustre to the often uninspiring proceedings.

Noi Tre (*Us Three*, 1984), directed by Pupi Avati

Loosely based on a series of events in 1770, this is a delicate and touching study of the last moments of childhood, as the young Mozart spends a summer with his father on a country estate, preparing for a music exam. Writer and director Avati shows Mozart as an ordinary boy – fighting with the local youth, engaging in an adolescent romance – while all the time he is aware of the siren call of genius, which he attempts to evade by making deliberate errors in the exam.

I Nuovi Angeli (*The New Angels*, 1961), directed by Ugo Gregoretti

Like all portmanteau films, Gregoretti's ambitious eight-part work is, like the curate's egg, better in some parts than in others. But as a study of Italy in the 1960s (with an emphasis on the young) the various tales often have a sharpness and insight that does full justice to the material. Utilising a non-professional cast, Gregoretti's documentary approach to his subject touches on a variety of classes, and sardonic humour rubs shoulders with more serious themes. While the piece has little application today, it is still an intriguing snapshot of the era in which it was made.

La Notte di San Lorenzo (*The Night of San Lorenzo*, 1981), directed by Paolo and Vittorio Taviani

The special jury prize at Cannes was awarded to the Taviani brothers' film in 1982, and it is among their most acclaimed pieces of work. As the Nazis get ready to destroy the Tuscan village of San Martino in 1944, a resistance group is organised, realising that the American advance will probably arrive too late. As the Liberation approaches, savage conflicts ensue, and a picture of Italian courage in the face of insurmountable odds is drawn. Using autobiographical elements from their own childhood, the Taviani brothers create sharp and poignant vignettes, notably those seen by the young girl who is foregrounded in the narrative. Not everything in the film wears well, but it is still a powerful experience.

Le Notti di Cabiria (*Nights of Cabiria*, 1956), directed by Federico Fellini

This bittersweet glimpse into the life and dreams of an unquenchably optimistic prostitute was Fellini's farewell to neorealism before embarking upon his more familiar, glitzier films. Giulietta Masina – Fellini's wife – had already appeared as the resilient prostitute in *Lo Sceicco Bianco* (*The White Sheik*) but now had a whole film for her episodic story of successive disillusionments from which she learns nothing. The film was later adapted into the Broadway musical *Sweet Charity*. The film has recently been digitally mastered from a restored print and now contains a seven-minute sequence not seen since the film's Cannes premiere.

Otello (1986), directed by Franco Zeffirelli

The response to Zeffirelli's film of Verdi's Shakespearean opera was sharply divided, and critical opinion has remained split ever since. From the musical point of view, the film is a cherishable record of one of the great modern Othellos, Placido Domingo, even if the supporting cast (Katia Ricciarelli as Desdemona and Justino Diaz as Iago) do not match his achievement.

The score was chopped about to some degree, and the director altered the order of incidents in the opera. It is possible, however, to be a little too precious about this; after all, Verdi himself took considerable liberties with Shakespeare's text and, in the interests of conveying a striking dramatic (and operatic) experience, Zeffirelli's playing fast and loose with the original is not the greatest of crimes.

Padre Padrone (1977), directed by Paolo and Vittorio Taviani

A Sardinian father despatches his son to the mountains to act as shepherd, despite his youthfulness. The boy grows up with no knowledge of any language, but education he accrues during his military service finally prepares him to make the all too necessary break from his parent. Gavino Ledda's autobiographical book provided strong material for the Taviani brothers to work from, and much of the incidental detail has a verisimilitude that always convinces. If at times the brothers are guilty of nudging the audience rather too obviously, it is a forgivable error. Certainly the jury at Cannes thought so in 1977, when they awarded *Padre Padrone* the best film prize.

Passione d'Amore (1981), directed by Ettore Scola

An intriguing cast (Laura Antonelli, Jean-Louis Trintignant and Massimo Girotti among others) are put through their paces in this slightly overwrought but entertaining drama in which an army captain, Giorgio, played by Bernard Giraudeau, finds his sex life curtailed when moved to another post, away from his mistress Clara (Antonelli). He finds himself fascinated by the unprepossessing Fosca (Valeria D'Obici), cousin of the local colonel. She appears to be ill and antisocial, but despite her forbidding manner and unlovely appearance, Giorgio becomes more and more fascinated by her. In many ways, Stephen Sondheim's Broadway musical *Passion*, a more recent version of this story, was far more subtle and intelligent in its treatment of a highly unorthodox subject. Nevertheless, it is an intriguing drama.

Il Posto (*The Job*, 1961), directed by Ermanno Olmi

One of the most engaging of Italian art films, this deeply sympathetic and brilliantly detailed piece maintains a modern appeal nearly 50 years after it was made. A young man, Sandro Panzeri, from an impoverished background succeeds in getting a job in a Milanese business, and works his way up through a succession of ever more responsible positions. Famously, the cast is entirely composed of Milanese office workers, apart from Panzeri, who gives a beautifully nuanced and often very funny performance. This was Olmi's second film, and as a picture of what work does to people it remains as telling as ever. What, of course, makes it a particular success is the way the director treats quotidian events in quotidian lives as if they are quite as interesting as grand opera – and he makes them so.

I Pugni in Tasca (*Fists in the Pocket*, 1965), directed by Marco Bellocchio

Bellocchio's celebrated film remains as arresting as on its first appearance in the mid-1960s, when it achieved nigh universal international acclaim. The family at the centre of the piece is a dysfunctional one: the blind mother (played by Liliona Gerace) deals with her children (including two epileptic brothers, and their deranged sister played by Paola Pitagora) while the one member of the family able to function normally, the resourceful Marino Masè, finds his attempts to live a normal life are constrained by his bizarre family. An escape is offered by his younger brother (Lou Castel), whose radical solution is to murder the other members of the family. As a picture of middle-class Italian society, Bellocchio's vision is as scarifying as one could wish, and even though the basic situation is (deliberately) unlikely, many cogent points are made about repression and the necessity of maintaining a 'correct' façade. For a film made when the director was in his early 20s, it is astonishingly assured. Bellocchio's bleakly comic study of bourgeois life was one of the most striking and masterly debuts of the Sixties and is enhanced by a powerful Ennio Morricone score.

Salo or the 120 Days of Sodom (*Salò o le 120 Giornate di Sodoma*, 1975), directed by Pier Paolo Pasolini

For long time, the very title of Pasolini's film was an index of the unacceptable in cinematic excess – a film so disturbing in its uncompromising violence and perverted sexuality that it seemed as if it would forever have censorship problems. The horrors of the last reel were famously among the most unsettling ever put on celluloid, all the more disturbing for the director's consummate skill; using sex as a metaphor for power. It is also a prophetic view of our contemporary corporate-run culture of consumerism. Drawing on the Marquis de Sade's original novel, the film depicts the series of sexual tortures inflicted by four libertines upon a group of young men and women. Unavailable in Britain for many years, *Salò* was finally passed uncut by the BBFC in late 2000.

Salon Kitty (1976), directed by Tinto Brass

For many years, Tinto Brass's Italo-German production Salon Kitty was only available in a heavily cut form, but nevertheless enjoyed considerable notoriety for its depiction of the sexual excesses of the Nazi regime (Brass's film is principally set in a brothel, staffed by girls of good Aryan stock and impeccable National Socialist credentials; the girls were used to worm secrets out of indiscreet clients). In fact, Salon Kitty begot an entire subgenre: the Italian Nazi excess movie, with a graphic sexuality of Brass's film shored up with equally unflinching violence. But now that a director's cut of Salon Kitty is available with nearly 18 minutes of censored material restored, it's possible to judge the director's intention, hopefully shaking off the excrescences that have gathered since the film's release.

How does it look in the twenty-first century? The good things first: it was a considerable coup for Tinto Brass to acquire as his set designer the man who bids fair to be the finest in the history of the cinema: Ken Adam, no less, fresh off turbulent work with Stanley Kubrick. His settings for this vision of a decadent Reich are full of his trademark glittering surfaces, uncluttered expanses and modernistic design; this is probably the film's key asset (as the sleeve cannily notes, along with 'frequent sex').

But Brass has another ace in the hole: the eponymous Kitty (the vulnerable Madam who takes on the corrupt Nazi Wallenberg played by Helmet Berger, in a replay of his role in Visconti's *The Damned*) is incarnated by one of the great actresses of the cinema, Ingrid Thulin, long one of the most reliable muses of Ingmar Bergman (before younger actresses such as Liv Ullman usurped her). Her performance is more mannered than her work for Bergman, but retains a pathetic dignity, appropriate in the face of the sexual shenanigans her character is ringmaster to. Another plus is the vocal dubbing of her Kurt Weill-like songs by the English jazz singer Annie Ross (past her best, but supplying the right Lotte Lenya-like note). And (probably best of all for most people) the restoration of the highly stylised, in-your-face eroticism that became the director's stock in trade is still eye-opening, even in the twenty-first century. The nudity is almost non-stop, and most of the orgies contains shots of labias and semi erections that really would have brought about the fall of Western society had we been allowed to see them.

On the debit side, there's a salutary reminder that Brass was never a sympathetic director of actors: most are encouraged to play full-out (including a Nazi officer who comically shouts every single line of his dialogue), and who labour under the disadvantage of acting in something other than their native language (this comprehensively sinks Helmut Berger's performance: his English simply isn't good enough – even in post-synch – to pass muster). So, a disappointment. Nevertheless, it's always a cause for celebration when censorship is routed, and a director's intentions (however dubious) are given their head – anyone who would argue with this proposition is a clearly not a cinema buff.

La Strada (*The Roads*, 1954), directed by Federico Fellini

Federico Fellini broke into the international scene with this poetic and personal tale of life with a travelling circus. In an unforgettable performance Giulietta Masina, Fellini's wife, plays the naive, exploited assistant and mistress to strongman Anthony Quinn, who ultimately realises her value to him.

Strategia del Ragno (*The Spider's Stratagem*, 1970), directed by Bernardo Bertolucci

A wondrously intelligent and densely allusive version of a Borges short story, transposed by Bertolucci to the Po Valley. Exquisitely shot by Vittorio Storaro, this complex riddle of a film follows the attempts of a young man to discover the truth about his dead father, whose memorial has been mysteriously defaced.

La Terra Trema (*The Earth Trembles*, 1948), directed by Luchino Visconti

An epic account of a Sicilian fishing community and the disasters encountered by a family who lose their boat in a storm. Although acted by non-professionals and avowedly Marxist, Visconti's inherent romanticism wins through in the monumental beauty of the images and operatic handling of character.

Theorem (*Teorema*, 1968), directed by Pier Paolo Pasolini

A wealthy Italian bourgeois family faces collapse after each of its members is seduced in turn by a mysterious Christ or Devil like stranger (Terence Stamp). This enigmatic fable is used by Pasolini to explore family dynamics and in particular the subversive power of homosexuality.

Voyage to Italy (*Viaggio in Italia*, 1953), directed by Roberto Rossellini

Ingrid Bergman and George Sanders star in this deceptively slight tale of a couple in a dissolving marriage travelling to Naples to sell their home. The journey and the experience of Italy, including Pompeii, sparks a reconciliation and a fresh awareness of possibilities, all of which is captured by Rossellini with spellbinding subtlety.

Key Film Stars

Gina Lollobrigida

Even before Sofia Loren, Gina Lollobrigida was the first major European star whose name became synonymous with earthy sexuality: her voluptuous appeal, soon to be copied by a whole host of other Italian actresses (Loren among them), seemed far more sensual and vital than the often bloodless charms of her English and American rivals. She was, of course, 'La Lollo', and had a remarkable career, in which some excellent movies rubbed shoulders with a host of truly execrable ones. There was a rivalry with Loren: although the latter probably had a more distinguished career, Lollobrigida prided herself on her superior English, although neither woman could have been said to be completely at ease in the language. Her career was truly international, and there was barely a major European country in which she did not make films. Unlike Loren, her range was more restricted, but she undoubtedly possessed masses of charisma, and her sexuality fairly leapt off the screen.

Lollobrigida was born in Subiaco near Rome in 1928. Along with her three sisters, she moved to Rome and studied for a time to be a commercial artist. Her 'Lana Turner discovered at Schwaab's drugstore' moment came when she was spotted by Mario Costa, the director of *The Street*, who persuaded her to take a screen test for the film *L'Elisir d'Amore* (1946), with the great baritone Tito Gobbi. Interestingly, her film career continued in this operatic strain for the same director and she appeared in *Folia per l'Opera* in 1947 (again with Gobbi, and another great singer, Beniamino Gigli) and 1948's *I Pagliacci*, once again with Gobbi. She was, needless to say, dubbed, not possessing a great singing voice. But other films quickly followed, such as *La Sposa Non Può Attendere* with Gino Cervi and *Alina* with Amadeo Nazzari, an unconvincing melodrama.

Her first appearance before international audiences was in the film *A Tale of Five Cities* (1951, with Bonar Colleano). By now she had married Milko Skofic, whose sensuous photographic studies of her were heavily promoted in magazines. She was supported by a famous connoisseur of pulchritudinous female beauty, Howard Hughes, who asked her to journey to Hollywood. For a time she languished, until Hughes put her under long-term contract. This actually had the effect of inhibiting her Hollywood career, but she continued to make films in Italy, such as *Amor Non Ho... Però... Però* (1951, with Renato Rascel) and a notable appearance in *La Città Si Difende* (1951), which was a marked improvement on her earlier work. Pietro Germi found more interesting layers in her persona than simply the pouting sex bomb, although she still made workaday appearances in such films as

Enrico Caruso: Leggenda di una Voce (1951), which was an attempt to make Ermanno Randi a new Mario Lanza (even though his voice was supplied for the film by Maria Callas's long-time tenor partner, Mario del Monico).

Recently, prints have resurfaced of one of her most attractive and colourful films of this period, the costume epic *Fanfan la Tulipe* (1952), with Gérard Philipe buckling a swash with all the abandon of a young Errol Flynn. If Lollobrigida's performance came as much from her ample décolletage as from any acting skills, she nevertheless made her heroine a creature of flesh and blood, when many actresses in similar parts were able to make little impression. One of her biggest American films was 1956's *Trapeze*. Here, Lollobrigida (wearing a provocative bustier) played opposite two fine slices of American beefcake, Burt Lancaster and Tony Curtis, although the film's appeal lay more in the visible charms of its stars than in anything director Carol Reed had to offer. Her stint as the eponymous Queen of Sheba in King Vidor's *Solomon and Sheba* (1959, opposite Yul Bryner) demonstrated something of her fire as an actress, but *Never So Few* (1960) made little impression, with a by-the-numbers performance from Frank Sinatra as her lover.

She had not, however, deserted the Italian cinema. *La Bellezza di Ippolita* (1962) had her as a prostitute in a blond wig, and *Venere Imperiale* (1963) was an unexciting historical epic with Stephen Boyd. She coasted on her charisma in *Woman of Straw* (1964) opposite an uninvolved Sean Connery and the scene-stealing

Ralph Richardson, but 1965's *Le Bambole* was a diverting spin on Boccaccio with Jean Sorel. Later films made little impression, and only 1988's *La Romana* (with Francesca Dellera) had much to offer; this, in fact, was a remake of a film she had appeared in earlier. If Lollobrigida made nothing as impressive in her career as Loren's film for De Sica, *Two Women*, she will be eternally ensconced in the public imagination with her rival as the two most voluptuously sexy actresses in Italian cinema.

Marcello Mastroianni

It's difficult in the twenty-first century to describe the impact that Marcello Mastroianni made on international audiences in *La Dolce Vita*. New prints of the film have demonstrated just how well Fellini's 1960 masterpiece has worn, but one of the most timeless elements in it is Mastroianni's cool and dispassionate performance as the easily manipulated journalist Marcello. His charismatic manner and exquisite good looks made him one of the great international stars, and his career as a leading man continued for many years, even though those looks began to coarsen fairly quickly with age.

Mastroianni was born in Fontana Liri in 1924, where his father was a cabinetmaker. The family moved from Turin to Rome, and Mastroianni studied as a draughtsman. After being sent by the Germans to a labour camp in northern Germany, he escaped and lived clandestinely in Venice, working as a commercial illustrator. His first experience in the film industry was as an accountant for Eagle Lion/Rank Films, but he had begun to act in a drama group that also included Fellini's wife Giulietta Massina. Visconti saw him in one of these productions and chose him to appear in a version of Shakespeare's *As You Like It*, which led to other performances in plays by Arthur Miller, Tennessee Williams and Chekov. One of his earliest film roles was in an adaptation of Hugo's *Les Miserables* (1948), but his first major role was in Luciano Emmer's *Una Domenica d'Agosto* (1950), which was a series of low-key observations (in documentary style) of a seaside Sunday. Several indifferent thrillers followed, although more impressive roles were just around the corner. His work with Sophia Loren and Vittoria De Sica in *Peccato che Sia una Canaglia* in 1954 made an impression, with this piece (adapted from a story by Alberto Moravia) full of character, along with a striking performance by Mastroianni.

But it was Mastroianni's performance for his discoverer, Visconti, in *Le Notti Bianche* (1957) that made a mark, despite the limitations of the film. This adaptation of Dostoyevsky also starred Jean Marais and Maria Schell. The year 1960 brought Mastroianni a career-defining performance in *La Dolce Vita*, discussed elsewhere. Repeated viewings convey the astonishing juggling act that is Mastroianni's performance here: at times he is a blank slate, simply the receptacle for the audience as it travels through the indulgences of the Roman jet set, but closer observation reveals a host of subtleties and nuances. At the same time, Mastroianni had appeared in the impressive *Adua e le Compagne*

(1960) as a small-time car salesman dallying with prostitute Simone Signoret, who (along with several of her fellow tarts) are attempting to open a restaurant. The film's strange mix of comedy and tragedy did not vitiate its considerable impact, and Mastroianni's performance was particularly notable, although, in retrospect, it is strange that he was still making cameo appearances like this when, at the same time, *La Dolce Vita* was to propel him to international stardom.

Having appeared for the most operatic of Italian directors in *La Dolce Vita*, Mastroianni was now cast in a film for the cool, analytical Michelangelo Antonioni. *La Notte* (1961) enshrines one of the actor's finest performances, very different from his Marcello in *La Dolce Vita* but equally buffeted by life's circumstances. Another major hit followed with Pietro Germi's *Divorzio all'Italiana* (1961), a broad but still funny comedy with Mastroianni as a Sicilian count trying hard to dump his overweight, moustachioed wife in an attempt to marry his beguiling cousin. Mastroianni won numerous awards for this, and managed to break out of the arthouse realm abroad. *Vie Privée* in 1962 for Louis Malle did little for Mastroianni's career – his relationship with co-star Brigitte Bardot struck few sparks in the movie – and it was Fellini's *8½* (1963) that reminded audiences how he was the perfect surrogate for the director (much in the same way as Max Von Sydow performed this function in the films of Ingmar Bergman).

By now, Mastroianni was managed by Carlo Ponti, who worked as assiduously for the actor as he did for his (Ponti's) wife, Sophia Loren. A variety of indifferent films followed from this association, such as the portmanteau *Ieri, Oggi, Domani* (1963), a film that achieved some international success but that appears thin and strained today. Similarly, Monicelli's *Casanova '70* (1965) has sunk without trace, although *La Decima Vittima* (also 1965), based on the science fiction novel *The Seventh Victim* by Robert Sheckley, has now achieved a considerable cult following and looks more timely than ever with its swingeing satire of reality TV very prescient indeed. As his career progressed, much of the sheen that had burnished his first successes was worn away by indifferent efforts such as *Gli Amanti* (1968), in which Mastroianni and Faye Dunaway calmly went through the motions of an unexciting relationship. His English in the film was unconvincing, principally as the actor had had to learn the part phonetically. Back in his native country, he appeared in *I Girasoli* (1970) with Sophia Loren, which made little impact, and his turn in the wildly inconsistent career of John Boorman for *Leo the Last* (1970) in Britain showed unfortunate timing, as this was one of the director's most misguided efforts.

Looking at Polanski's *What?* (1973) today is a strange experience. This sex comedy in the surrealist Terry Southern vein has its moments, but Mastroianni's mugging, over-the-top performance is not one of its virtues. However, Marco Ferreri's *La Grande Bouffe* (1973), which shocked audiences in its day, has a striking performance by the actor as one of a group of suicidal, indulgent men, propelling themselves to destruction through orgies of sexual excess and food.

Mauro Bolognini's *Per le Antiche Scale* in 1975 showcased another well-drawn Mastroianni performance, and, despite a slew of indifferent films, he worked once again with the director who had done the most favours for him, Federico Fellini, in *Ginger e Fred* (1986) with Giulietta Massina, and slipped into mugging mode once again for Altman in *Prêt-à-Porter* (1994). As the years passed, Mastroianni's indifferent films and bad performances (and there are many of both) seemed to slip away and his glorious, insightful work for such directors as Fellini and Antonioni looks more timeless and provocative than ever.

Monica Vitti

The thriller writer Peter O'Donnell could not believe his luck when he learned that the woman who was to incarnate his sexy, intelligent heroine Modesty Blaise on film was to be no less than Monica Vitti, the sexy, charismatic muse of such directors as Antonioni. And the Modesty film was to be directed by Joseph Losey, with Dirk Bogarde as the villain – how could it fail? O'Donnell now groans at any mention of the movie, and one of the many reasons for its failure is, of course, Vitti. She appears briefly in the film in a black catsuit and dark wig that makes her the epitome of O'Donnell's heroine, but the actress's laziness (shamelessly indulged by the director) pretty much sinks Modesty without trace. However, truly bad movies by Vitti do not remain in the mind. Mostly, we think of her as the fascinating centre of a selection of remarkable movies directed by Antonioni, for whom she was the perfect muse.

When in 1957 she performed dubbing chores for the actress Dorian Grey in *Il Grido*, she ran into Antonioni, who was to change her life. Vitti had been born in Rome in 1931 (her real name was Maria Luisa Ceciarelli), and she had made a promising start in the Accademia d'Arte Drammatica in Rome. Small film roles in undistinguished comedies with actors such as Ugo Tognazzi had made little impact, but when she started to work with the director (on such plays as *I am a Camera*) the director began to plot her career in much the same way as Hitchcock had done with actresses like Grace Kelly and Vera Miles.

L'Avventura (1960) of course was the signature film for Antonioni and Vitti, a masterpiece that established the duo in a similar fashion to the teaming of Mastroianni and Fellini in *La Dolce Vita*. The film was shot in Sicily and the Ligurian islands, and Vitti's performance (eschewing all the dramatic tics that had been the standard both in Hollywood and at Cinecittà) represented a new kind of film acting. It is the cool, underplayed neurosis of many of her roles for Antonioni that looks as modern as ever today, with the refusal to rely on any kind of artificial dramatic semaphore. The actress's interior life seems quite as rich and convincing as anything played by graduates of the Stella Adler/Lee Strasbourg schools. Her performance in Antonioni's *La Notte* (1961) was equally striking, though the role was a small one: the film belonged to Marcello Mastroianni and Jeanne Moreau as the estranged couple attempting to find some meaning in their lives. One of the director's most controversial films, *L'Eclisse* (1962), followed, with Vitti involved with energetic stock broker Alain Delon, trying to protect her stock market-obsessed mother. There are those who regard the film as one of Antonioni's great masterpieces, but there is no denying that a certain application is required to fully appreciate it. Similarly, there were those who thought that Vitti's acting style was now turning into mannerism, but the film today gives the lie to that: her character in *L'Eclisse* is subtly different from characterisations she had given us before.

Work for other directors followed, such as the French *Les Quatre Vérités* in 1962, which was an overwrought comedy with Rossano Brazzi, and Roger Vadim's *Château en Suède* (1963), where her supposedly bewitching character actually looked drained and uncharismatic. But appearing in Antonioni's first film in colour, *Il Deserto Rosso* (1964), as yet another in the director's gallery of alienated heroines, showed that she remained as fascinating a screen presence as ever, even though her character's actions (in relation to a lip-synched Richard Harris) are often as infuriating as they are intriguing. A comedy with Tony Curtis, *La Cintura di Castità* (1968) followed and made little impression, then the Modesty Blaise debacle which did nothing for the careers of anyone involved. Other choices seem similarly uninspired, such as Ettore Scola's *Dramma della Gelosia – Tutti i Particolari in Cronaca* in 1970, in which neither she nor Mastroianni could make much of an indifferent script. Later work in her career still showed the skills that had distinguished her debut movies, such as Miklós Jansco's *La Pacifista* (1970), where her performance as a TV journalist made a mark, and she turned once again to the stage, appearing in Neil Simon's distaff version of his *The Odd Couple*.

The popular image of Vitti is of a cool, restrained, intellectual sexuality, very different from the earthy charms of Loren and Lollobrigida. If Joan Baker was England's thinking man's crumpet, Vitti undoubtedly deserves that non-PC epithet for her own country, but there was much more to her than a slightly glacial sex appeal, Vitti's performances in a variety of excellent movies demonstrate that she was one of the most considerable actresses of the Italian screen.

Sophia Loren

Born in Rome in 1934, Sophia Loren and her mother moved to Naples, where she spent the early years of her childhood in less than salubrious conditions. At the age of 14, she won a beauty contest, which prompted her ambitious mother to take her back to Rome and try for a film career. The *fumetti* (comic strips illustrated with photographs) were enjoying their greatest popularity at the time, and Loren was a natural for these, with her impressive figure assuring her a stream of work. Small parts in films quickly followed, and even before her greatest success as an actress she had met her future husband, the producer Carlo Ponti. She had worked with Silvana Mangano, but while that actress was to achieve a breakthrough in *Riso Amaro*, Loren's ultimate success was to be more long-lasting, and was to have an international dimension that Mangano barely enjoyed. By now, Ponti had begun to shape her career, and facilitated her starring in a film of Verdi's *Aida* (1953 – where her voice was supplied by the great soprano Renata Tebaldi). The film today looks great indeed, and other early movies, such as *Un Giorno in Pretura* (1954 – with Alberto Sordi), give little hint of the seductive charisma that was to propel her later.

Noting that Mangano's provocatively dishevelled clothing in *Riso Amaro* had made such an international impact, Carlo Ponti ensured that Loren performed a similar trick in *La Donna del Fiume* (1954), in which her voluptuous charms were barely concealed by sketchy (and sometimes wet) apparel. The film (despite crass dubbing) enjoyed some success abroad, and began the ascent to fame that was soon to gather considerable momentum. American films soon followed, such as *Boy on a Dolphin* (1957), co-starring Alan Ladd, which once again gave Loren a chance to dive into water (this time as a Greek peasant woman) and allow the camera to record every inch of her opulent charms. But the film added little lustre to any opinion of her acting talents. Similarly, the ill-fated *The Pride and the Passion* (1957), with a temperamental Frank Sinatra matching Loren's fieriness, was one of Stanley Kramer's least interesting films. Carlo Ponti, however, had not given up on the idea of his wife appearing in more ambitious films, such as the 1958 attempt at Eugene O'Neill's *Desire Under the Elms* with Burl Ives and Anthony Perkins. This film conveyed much of Loren's dramatic power as an actress, often sidelined in more workaday productions, although it seems unlikely that Loren could convey the requisite subtlety for the part on stage.

Other Hollywood work called upon Loren to be more of an iconic presence than anything else; one of Hollywood's most talented and individual directors, Anthony Mann, called on this aspect from Loren in *El Cid* (1961), made in Spain, but a return to Italy and the De Sica episode of *Boccaccio 70* (also 1962) showed that the earthy ebullience of Loren's Italian films had not vanished under a Hollywood gloss. Hopes were high for *I Sequestrati di Altona* (1962), De Sica's version of Sartre's play *The Condemned of Altona*, but the film itself was a worthy and unexciting run-through of the Sartre drama. But De Sica was to provide the actress with one of the parts of her career in *La Ciociara* (1960), a version of Alberto Moravia's *Two Women*, with Loren devastating as a widow in an Italy riven by war; the rape of the Loren character and her daughter and its aftermath were handled with a power that surfaced all too infrequently in the actress's career. Loren won the best actress award at Cannes and the first ever Oscar for best actress in a foreign-language film; all fully deserved, although the film itself had been distributed abroad in a poorly dubbed version.

Other unimpressive American films such as *Judith* (1966) followed, and an end-of-cycle entry in the Hitchcock pastiche stakes, *Arabesque* (1966) with Gregory Peck. Chaplin's *A Countess from Hong Kong* (1967) augured well, with the actress as the decent noblewoman sexually involved with Marlon Brando, but none of the participants cover themselves in glory. Even poorer films followed, such as the disastrously dull version of the hit Broadway musical *Man of La Mancha* (1972), with Loren and Peter O'Toole making nothing of their parts. And it is best to draw a veil over the ill-conceived remake of *Brief Encounter* (1974) with Richard Burton. The idea of Burton and Loren, glamorous superstars, replacing the more quotidian Trevor Howard and Celia Johnson is absurd enough even as a concept, and the film proved such misgivings all too prescient. After such plodding thrillers as *The Cassandra Crossing* in 1977, Loren began an astonishingly misconceived vanity project, a film for television called *Sophia Loren: Her Own Story* (1980), a version of her autobiography with the actress playing herself as the mature Loren and even her own mother, while Ritza Brown played the younger Loren. By now Loren was in danger of removing all the goodwill her earlier films had accrued, but she will always remain the best known of the great Italian film stars.

Anna Magnani

From her humble birth in Alexandria near the beginning of the twentieth century, Anna Magnani's life trajectory was to be a preparation for her greatest roles in the cinema. Brought up in a shabby suburb of Rome, she decided to break out of the poverty of her environment by applying to study at the Corso Eleanora Dusa at Santa Cecilia, but kept body and soul together by performing near-the-knuckle songs in music halls. Her entré into the world of films came after her meeting with film director Goffredo Alessandrini, who married her in 1933 (although, in fact, the marriage did not last). Her first film was a career-making role as a 'kept woman' in *La Cieca di Sorrento* (1934). She also appeared as a music hall performer in the film *Cavalleria* in 1936, a jaundiced vision of upper-crust Italian society.

As Magnani slowly began to build her film career she was simultaneously taking the career path that had made the name of so many of the better film actors (as opposed to stars) – success on the stage. Her performance in Eugene O'Neill's *Anna Christie* was much applauded, but films such as *La Fugitiva* in 1941 added little lustre to her career. Vittorio De Sica was one of the film directors who saw her potential and cast her in *Teresa Venerdì* (1941), where a hint of her opulent eroticism made a mark with critics and audiences. Several workaday films followed, and slowly but surely she established her name as a star. Interestingly, she undertook the part that many other non-operatic actresses have essayed in Italian cinema, as a Tosca figure in *Avanti a Lui Tremava Tutta Roma* (1946) opposite Tito Gobbi, who made a speciality of such films. Her singing voice was, of course, dubbed. An early film of which she could be proud was Alberto Lattuada's *Il Bandito* (1946), in which Magnani inveigles Amadeo Nazzari into a criminal lifestyle, much in the fashion that Carmen performs the same function for Don José.

Vittorio Cottafavi, later to make one of the most imaginative of the Hercules films in *Ercole alla Conquista di Atlantide*, cast her with Vittorio De Sica in *Lo Sconosciuto di San Marino* (1946), but this, like many of her early films, was made for domestic consumption only. For Luigi Zappa she made the first film that was to impress foreign audiences, *L'Onorevole Angelina* (1947), which gained for her the best actress award at Venice, and also created something of a critical stir in both the UK and America.

While the Production Code was forcing a ludicrous innocence on American product at the time (directors such as Michael Curtiz was forced to subvert such code pronouncements as, re Bogart and Bergman in *Casablanca*, 'there must be no suggestion of a sex affair'), Magnani, like so many continental actresses, could deal with the realities of life, erotic or otherwise, in a more frank and honest way — although, inevitably, when the films travelled abroad they were often mauled by censors. Such a case was Roberto Rossellini's *L'Amore* (1948), a two-part film, one half of which was Cocteau's *La Voix Humain*, while the Magnani segment (*Il Miracolo*) had the actress as a peasant woman who is raped and becomes convinced that her child will be the Messiah. The film was mangled abroad, and its US showing under the title *The Miracle* upset the censor. But Magnani and Rossellini had established a relationship (under threat when Rossellini began an affair with Ingrid Bergman). Magnani's best work for Rossellini was, of course, in one of the great Italian neorealist masterpieces, *Roma, Città Aperta* (1945), where her tragic performance was almost combustible in the context of this bleak and powerful film.

Visconti's *Bellissima* in 1951 was a lively and energetic comedy, with Magnani as a stage mother forcing her child into a film career. She worked for Jean Renoir in *The Golden Coach* in 1953, another film made in a variety of versions. But now an international career beckoned, with one of her most memorable roles in the film of Tennessee Williams's *The Rose Tattoo* (1955). She had previously been approached to do the play on Broadway – the role of a volatile Italian woman having an affair with an inarticulate, brutish truck driver seemed tailor-made for her. She was, however, persuaded to make the film version. Opposite Burt Lancaster, she instantly established her international career, winning an Oscar as best actress and numerous other awards (including the BFA award and the New York Critics' award). *Wild is the Wind* (1957) continued her American career as a mail-order bride for Anthony Quinn; although directed by the most distinguished of 'women's' directors, George Cukor, this was only fitfully successful, as was her next Tennessee Williams' film *The Fugitive Kind* in 1960, in which she played a sexually frustrated store owner who seduces a fey, guitar-playing young man. Although Williams wrote the part for her (and tailored it to her specialities as an actress), and although the casting of Marlon Brando promised fireworks between the stars, the film has not worn well and looks artificial and pretentious today.

Another great part remained for the actress, to be provided by one of the most promising young directors of the time, the Marxist and homosexual Paolo Pasolini. *Mamma Roma*, in 1962, starred the actress as a prostitute prepared to make any sacrifice for her worthless, petty hoodlum son. If Pasolini was inclined to indulge the actress, and some of her mannerisms are allowed to become too strident, there is no denying the sheer incandescence of her performance, which looks impressive even today. She followed this with an Italian TV series, *Made in Italy* (1966), which, despite the presence of several impressive Italian actors, was not seen much abroad. An indifferent Hollywood effort followed in Stanley Kramer's *The Secret of Santa Vittoria* in 1969, again with Anthony Quinn. Both stars almost contrived to rise above their material, but her last impressive appearance was a cameo playing herself in Fellini's nostalgic *Roma* in 1972.

At her death in 1973, her stock had fallen somewhat, and her kind of flamboyant (though truthful) acting had fallen out of favour, but there are signs of a critical reassessment, and her best work is now being looked upon once again with favour.

Index

1900/Novecento, 128
8½, 44, 46, 47, 49, 142

Accatone, 53, 54
Adua e le Compagne/Hungry for Love, 141
Africa Addio, 104
Aida, 148
Alina, 138
All the Colours of Darkness/Tutti i Colori del Buio, 69
Allegro Non Troppo, 104
Amanti, Gli, 143
Amici per la Pelle/Friends for Life, 105
Amor Non Ho… Però… Però, 138
Amore, L', 152
Année Dernière à Marienbad, L'/Last Year at Marienbad, 36
Arabian Nights, The/Il Fiore delle Mille e Una Notti, 106
Arizona Si Scattenò… e Li Fece Fuori Tutti, 70
Assassino, L'/The Assassin, 106
Assedio di Alcazar, L'/The Siege of Alcazar, 14
Avanti a Lui Tremava Tutta Roma, 151
Avventura, L', 39, 40, 123, 145

Bambini Ci Guardano, I/The Children Are Watching Us, 24
Bambole, Le, 140
Bandito, Il, 151
Bandits at Orgosolo, The/I Banditi a Orgosolo, 107
Baron Blood/Gli Orrori del Castello di Norimberga, 56, 57
Battle of Algiers, The/La Battaglia di Algeri, 107
Before the Revolution/Prima della Rivoluzione, 108
Bellezza di Ippolita, La, 139
Bellissima, 153
Beyond, The/L'Aldilà, 60

INDEX

Bird with the Crystal Plumage, The/L'Uccello dalle Piume di Cristallo, 62, 70, 98
Black Belly of the Tarantula, The/La Tarantola dal Ventre Nero, 77
Black Sabbath, 73
Black Sunday/La Maschera del Demonio, 55, 56, 57
Blade of the Ripper, 70
Blood and Black Lace/Sei Donne per l'Assassino, 57, 75, 76
Blow Up, 39, 63
Boccaccio 70, 51, 149

Cabiria, 11, 12
Caccia Tragica/Tragic Pursuit, 32, 34
Caduta di Troia, La/The Fall of Troy, 11
Cannibal Ferox/Make Them Die Slowly, 71, 72
Canterbury Tales, The/I Racconti di Canterbury, 106, 108
Casanova '70, 143
Case of the Scorpion's Tail, The/La Coda dello Scorpione, 70
Caso Mattei, Il/The Mattei Affair, 109
Cavalleria, 151
Cavalleria Rusticana, 19
Christ Stopped at Eboli/Cristo si e Fermato a Eboli, 110
Cieca di Sorrento, La, 151
Cinema Paradiso, 110

Cintura di Castità, La, 146
Ciociara, La, 149
Città Si Difende, La, 138
City of the Living Dead/Paura nella Città dei Morti Viventi, 60
City of Women/La Città delle Donne, 111
Cold Eyes of Fear, The/Gli Occhi Freddi della Paura, 79
Companeros, 98, 99
Condemned of Altona, The/I Sequestrati di Altona, 149
Conformista, Il/The Conformist, 111
Conversation Piece/Gruppo di Famiglia in un Interno, 112
Cristo Proibito, Il/The Forbidden Christ, 53
Cronaca di un Amore/Story of a Love Affair, 35, 36
Cronaca di una Morte Annunciata/Chronicle of a Death Foretold, 113
Cronaca Familiare/Family Diary, 113
Cynic, the Rat and the Fist, The/Il Cinico, l'Infame e il Violento, 72

Death Carries a Cane/Passi di Danza su una Lama di Rasoio, 79
Death in Venice/Morte a Venezia, 33, 114
Death Laid an Egg/La Morte Ha Fatto l'Uovo, 80

INDEX

Death Occurred Last Night/La Morte Risale a Ieri Sera, 114
Decameron, The/Il Decamerone, 106, 108, 115
Decima Vittima, La, 143
Deep Red/Profondo Rosso, 62, 63, 83
Deserto Rosso, Il/Red Desert, 39, 42, 131, 146
Divorce Italian Style/Divorzio all'Italiana, 116
Django, 97, 98, 100, 101
Dolce Vita, La, 44, 45, 46, 51, 75, 140, 141, 142, 145
Domenica d'Agosto, Una, 141
Don't Torture a Duckling/Non Si Sevezia un Paperino, 81
Donna del Fiume, La, 148
Dramma della Gelosia – Tutti i Particolari in Cronaca, 146
Dreamers, The, 103

Eaten Alive/Mangiati Vivi dai Cannibali, 71, 72
Eclisse, L'/The Eclipse, 39, 40, 41, 43, 146
Ecology of a Crime/A Bay of Blood/Bloodbath/Twitch of the Death Nerve/Ecologia del Delitto, 75, 76
Elisir d'Amore, L', 138
Enrico Caruso: Leggenda di una Voce, 139

Famiglia, La/The Family, 117
Fellini Satyricon, 46, 117
Fidanzati, I/The Engagement, 116

Fistful of Dollars, A/Un Pugno di Dollari, 89, 100
Fistful of Dynamite, A/Duck, You Sucker!/Once Upon a Time...The Revolution/Giu la Testa, 93, 94
Folia per l'Opera, 138
For a Few Dollars More/Per Qualche Dollaro in Piu, 90
Forbidden Photos of a Lady Above Suspicion, The/Le Foto Probite di una Signora per Bene, 81
Four Days of Naples, The/Le Quattro Giornate di Napoli, 118
Four Flies on Grey Velvet/Quattro Mosche di Velluto Grigio, 82
Free Hand for a Tough Cop/Il Trucido e lo Spirro, 72
Fugitiva, La, 151

Garden of the Finzi-Continis, The/Il Giardino dei Finzi-Contini, 118
Gente del Po, La/The People of the Po, 35
Germania, Anno Zero/Germany, Year Zero, 19, 22, 23
Ginger e Fred, 144
Giorno in Pretura, Un, 148
Girasoli, I, 143
Girl Friends, The/Le Amiche, 119
Giulietta degli Spiriti/Juliet of the Spirits, 46, 50

INDEX

Gli Ultimi Giorni di Pompei/The Last Days of Pompeii, 11
Golden Coach, The/La Carrozza d'Oro, 120, 153
Good, the Bad and the Ugly, The/Il Buono, il Brutto, il Cattivo, 91, 92
Gospel According to Saint Matthew, The/Il Vangelo Secondo Matteo, 121
Gramigna's Lover, 17
Great Silence/Il Grande Silenzio, 98
Grido, Il/The Cry, 37, 38, 39, 45, 145

Hands over the City/Le Mani sulla Citta, 122
Hercules Conquers Atlantis/Ercole alla Conquista di Atlantide, 58
Hercules in the Haunted World/Ercole al Centro della Terra, 58
Hercules Unchained/Ercole e la Regina di Lidia, 58
Hercules/La Fatiche di Ercole, 58
Horrible Secret of Dr Hichcock, The.L'Orribile Segreto di Dr Hichcock, 73
House by the Cemetery, The/Quella Villa Accanto al Cimitero, 61
House of Exorcism/La Casa dell'Esorcismo, 56
House with the Laughing Windows, The/La Casa dalle Finestre che Ridono, 78

Identification of a Woman/Identificazione di una Donna, 122, 123
Ieri, Oggi, Domani, 143
Iguana with a Tongue of Fire, The/L'Iguana dalla Lingua di Fuoco, 83
Inferno, 63, 64, 66
Innocente, L'/The Innocent, 123
Investigation of a Citizen above Suspicion/Indagine su un Cittadino al di Sopra di Ogni Sospetto, 124
Island of the Fish Men, 70

Killer Must Kill Again, The, 67, 71
Kriminal, 71

Ladri di Biciclette/Bicycle Thieves, 19, 25, 26, 27, 30, 52
Leopard, The, 37, 41, 42, 48, 112
Lisa and the Devil, 56
Lizard in a Woman's Skin, A/Una Lucertola nella Pelle di una Donna, 59, 84

Ma l'Amore Mio Non Muore/Love Everlasting, 13
Made in Italy, 154

INDEX

Mamma Roma, 125, 153
Man Called Blade,
   A/Mannaha, 70
Man of Straw/L'Uomo di
   Paglia, 125
Manhattan Baby/Possessed,
   58, 59
Medea, 126
Mercenary, The/A Professional
   Gun/Il Mercanario, 98
Mille Peccati... Nessuna
   Virtù/A Thousand Sins and
   No Virtue, 68
Minnesota Clay, 100
Miserables, Les/I Miserabili,
   141
Mondo Cane, 68, 104

Navajo Joe/Un Dollaro a
   Testa, 100
New York Ripper, The/Lo
   Squartatore di New York,
   86
Nightmare City/Incubo sulla
   Citta Contaminata, 72
Noi Tre/ Us Three, 126
Nome della Legge, In/In the
   Name of the Law, 44
Notte di San Lorenzo, La/
   The Night of San Lorenzo,
   127
Notte, La/The Night, 39, 40,
   123, 142, 145
Notti Bianche, Le, 141
Notti di Cabiria, Le/Nights of
   Cabiria, 128
Nuovi Angeli, I/The New
   Angels, 127

Once Upon a Time in America,
   92, 96
Once Upon a Time in the
   West/C'era una Volta il
   West, 90, 92, 93, 95
Onorevole Angelina,
   L'/Angelina, 152
Ossessione/Obsession, 15, 16,
   32, 33, 36, 37
Otello, 128

Pacifista, La, 147
Padre Padrone, 129
Pagliacci, I, 19, 138
Paisa, 44
Palio, 14
Passenger, The/Professione
   Reporter, 39
Passione d'Amore, 129
Peccato che Sia una Canaglia,
   141
Per le Antiche Scale, 144
Pilota Ritorna, Un/A Pilot
   Returns, 15, 34
Posto, Il/The Job, 130
Presa di Roma, La/The Taking
   of Roma, 10
Prova d'Orchestra/Orchestral
   Rehearsal, 48
Pugni in Tasca, I/Fists in the
   Pocket, 131

Ragazzi dei Parioli, I, 68
Ringo and His Golden
   Pistol/Johnny Oro,
   100
Riso Amaro/Bitter Rice, 9,
   19, 32, 147, 148

INDEX

Roma, 46, 48, 154
Roma, Città Aperta/Rome, Open City, 14, 19, 20, 23, 44, 152
Romana, La, 140
Rotaie/Rails, 14

Salo or the 120 Days of Sodom/Salo o le 120 Giornate di Sodoma, 132
Salon Kitty, 132
Sceicco Bianco, Lo/The White Sheik, 44, 128
Sciuscia/Shoeshine, 19, 24, 26, 30
Sconosciuto di San Marino, Lo, 152
Scorpion with Two Tails, The/Murder in the Etruscan Cemetary/Assassinio all'Cimitero Etrusco, 71
Secret of Santa Vittoria, The, 154
Serpente, Il/The Serpent, 13
Sesso con un Sorriso/Sex with a Smile, 69
Seven Bloodstained Orchids/Sette Orchidee Macchiate Rosso, 71
Shock, 57
Slave, The, 97
So Sweet... So Perverse/Cosi Dolce... Cosi Perversa, 71
Sole/Sun, 14
Spasmo, 72
Sposa Non Può Attendere, La, 138

Strada, La, 45, 134
Strange Vice of Mrs Wardh, The, 70
Strategia del Ragno, La/The Spider's Strategem, 134
Street, The, 138
Suspiria, 38, 63, 64, 65, 66

Tale of Five Cities, A, 138
Tenebrae, 66
Teresa Venerdì, 151
Terra Trema, La/The Earth Trembles, 27, 135
Theorem/Teorema, 135
Torso/The Bodies Present Traces of Carnal Violence/I Corpi Presantano Tracce di Violenza Carnale, 69
Two Women, 140, 149

Umberto D, 26, 27, 35

Venere Imperiale, 139
Vitelloni, I, 45, 54
Voyage to Italy/Viaggio in Italia, 136

Whip and the Body, The/La Frusta e il Corpo, 70

Yeux Sans Visage, Les/Eyes Without a Face, 38

Zabriskie Point, 39
Zombie Flesh Eaters/Zombi 2, 60